PRAISE FOR *Youth Ministry as Peace Education*

"One of the greatest challenges of our time is finding ways of living together centered on peace, justice, and well-being. *Youth Ministry as Peace Education* is a much-needed resource most particularly because it effectively reminds parents, pastors, and activists that young people must and desire to be part of this effort. The book appropriately invites adults' serious reflections on prevailing disempowering views of youth. It presents varied forthright, creative, usable, theologically supported, and biblically informed practices for use in youth ministry to affirm the role of youth and empower their engagement."

—Anne E. Streaty Wimberly, executive director of Youth Hope-Builders Academy and Connecting With Hope Innovation Hub, Young Adult Ministry Initiative, Interdenominational Theological Center, Atlanta, GA

"*Youth Ministry as Peace Education* is the very best book on youth ministry I have ever read. Richly biblical, deeply formative, and beautifully written, it is also brilliantly educational and utterly practical. Read it together in communities of youth and adults and engage in the book's suggested activities. Absorb its wisdom and it will change your lives."

—Craig Dykstra, former senior vice president for religion at Lilly Endowment Inc., Indianapolis, IN; former professor of Christian education at Louisville Presbyterian Seminary, Princeton Theological Seminary, and Duke Divinity School

"Deliberate, liberative, intentional, democratic, and gospel-informed youth ministry. Rarely do books on youth ministry provide such profoundly captivating and pragmatic guidance for youth ministry. *Youth Ministry as Peace Education* is not only helpful for youth ministers but teaches how youth ministers can hold themselves accountable to the gospel, to modern-day social justice issues, and most importantly, to the youth they serve. Corrie provides youth ministers a field guide grounded in embodied research practices that boldly imagines a church where the youth are not just a program but the heartbeat of the community."

—Patrick B. Reyes, senior director of learning design, Forum for Theological Exploration; author of *The Purpose Gap*

"Corrie is a star among progressive youth ministry writers. *Youth Ministry as Peace Education* brings together her [Corrie's] deep respect for young people and her commitment to what Paulo Freire called 'education as a practice of freedom.' Readers also benefit from Corrie's expertise in interpreting Scripture, her passion for supporting youth engagement in the church's justice and peace work, and above all, her remarkable gifts as an educator who generously offers the blueprints for the Youth Theological Initiative's tried-and-true practices of youth ministry as peace education. A remarkable, practical, and readable volume."

—Joyce Ann Mercer, Bushnell Professor of Divinity, Yale Divinity School

"In *Youth Ministry as Peace Education*, Corrie draws from interdisciplinary resources and decades of teaching experience to amplify the voices of youth and disrupt the age-old trope that 'young people are to be seen and not heard.' This text increases the volume, so readers can hear young people whispering from the shadows of scriptural texts and clamoring for recognition in nineteenth-century psychology. She turns our attention to the outcries of youth activists seeking justice for immigrants, marching for Black lives, and addressing climate change. Yet I cherish most the clearly outlined strategies to aid educators, ministers, and parents who seek to create spaces for hard, heartfelt conversations with youth."

—Gregory C. Ellison II, associate professor of pastoral care and counseling, Candler School of Theology; founder of Fearless Dialogues

"Through all the years I've worked with youth, this is the book I've been missing. Biblically rooted, anchored by the insights and experiences of youth, and richly informed by theories of nonviolence and interculturality, Corrie guides readers in the practical cultivation of ministry that holds the potential to form youth and transform communities in the shape of compassion, peace, and justice. I've never read anything like it. This is an essential guide for all who are privileged to companion youth on the journey of becoming peace builders and justice seekers."

—Cody J. Sanders, American Baptist chaplain to Harvard University; author of *A Brief Guide to Ministry with LGBTQIA Youth*

"Elizabeth Corrie's *Youth Ministry as Peace Education* is a tour de force. She raises questions about the underlying assumptions many have about young people and reminds us to see youth in their rightful, prophetic, and peace-building roles. Corrie builds on years of peace-building justice work with youth and critical reflection on theology and culture to offer parents, pastors, and youth workers practical wisdom for a new vision of youth ministry that is hopeful and excited about the future with youth and young adults as engaged leaders in the struggles against violence and injustice."

—Almeda M. Wright, author of *The Spiritual Lives of Young African Americans*; associate professor of religious education, Yale Divinity School

"Corrie's *Youth Ministry as Peace Education* challenges youth ministry leaders to reimagine the capability of young people to become prophetic peacemakers. It illuminates the theological foundations and practices of one of the foremost practical theologians in the country. Every church and every youth leader should have a copy of this book. I'll be using it in my undergraduate and graduate youth ministry courses."

—Jeffrey Kaster, Saint John's School of Theology and Seminary, Collegeville, MN

"It is rare to encounter a book on youth ministry that doesn't position young people as a problem to be solved or a population to be saved. Corrie instead takes as her premise that young people are companions, citizens, and coconspirators in working actively to establish God's shalom. Through engagement with wide-ranging conversation partners—from deliberative democracy and strategies of nonviolent social change to liturgical formation and biblical exegesis—she [Corrie] describes and advocates for a youth ministry that is worthy of the young people who give themselves to it. Through her stories and examples, we capture a vision of how young people might be actively entrusted with the most important struggles, questions, and responsibilities of a life of faith."

—Katherine Turpin, professor of practical theology and religious education, Iliff School of Theology; author of *Nurturing Different Dreams: Youth Ministry across Lines of Difference*

"Drawing on over two decades of her own experience teaching and leading religious education with young people—along with fresh biblical scholarship, political theology, and cultural studies—Corrie has given the church a map for genuine accompaniment with youth as full members of the body of Christ. Her [Corrie's] vision for youth ministry should be our vision for the church at large as signs of and partners in God's mission of healing and liberation for the whole creation through practices that form disciples for the work of justice and peace. This book will be a tremendous asset for parents, youth workers, ministerial leaders, and seminary educators."

—Erik Christensen, pastor to the community and director of worship, Lutheran School of Theology at Chicago

"Corrie has worked hard to become the master of many apprenticing youth ministry workers, and this guidebook to her work is both travelogue and hitching post for anyone attempting to do the work. Corrie knows the heart of young people and the heart of God—and she recognizes those two are often comingled and intertwined. You would do best to sit, read, and learn from the best of the best."

—Robert W. Lee, pastor; author of *A Sin by Any Other Name: Reckoning with Racism and the Heritage of the South*

"*Youth Ministry as Peace Education* is a biblically inspired and theologically robust guide and resource to equip youth for the life-changing experience of being co-learners, fellow citizens, and members of the body of Christ in ministries of love, peace, and justice in their congregations and communities."

—Charles R. Foster, professor of religion and education emeritus, Candler School of Theology, Emory University; coauthor with Grant Shockley of *Working with Black Youth: Opportunities for Christian Ministry*; author of *From Generation to Generation: The Adaptive Challenge of Mainline Protestant Education in Forming Faith*

"Corrie provides the field guide we need for ministry with youth in the twenty-first century. She helps us notice, name, and nurture what young people—our *fellow citizens*—truly care about and what they're already doing with their lives that matters now. Each chapter is a gem of Christian practical wisdom and bold teaching strategies that inspire gospel-shaped civic action for the common good. A must-have book for cultivating a community of disciples of all ages!"

—Don C. Richter, author of *Mission Trips That Matter: Embodied Faith for the Sake of the World*

"For nearly three decades, the Youth Theological Initiative (YTI) at Emory University has hosted a premiere program engaging high school youth in exploring the intersections of Christian faith and justice. Corrie has been at the center of YTI's work for most of that time—working with youth, training staff, teaching, and developing curriculum. In this book, Corrie articulates her love for youth, justice, and peace that has been at the heart of this program. Her vision is crucial for the life of the church, the hurting world, and young people who yearn to find their place in God's world."

—David F. White, C. Ellis Nelson Professor of Christian Education, Austin Presbyterian Theological Seminary; author of *Practicing Discernment with Youth*; coeditor of *Joy: A Guide for Youth Ministry*; editor of *Journal of Youth and Theology*

"Youth ministry in 2021 looks very different from in the past. Impacted by the COVID-19 pandemic; fights against racism, homophobia, and sexism; and technology and the rise of misinformation, our young people are living in a world they are expected to shape while they fight to survive. Corrie is not only a guide for those of us in the midst of the work but a friend with whom to travel these uncharted roads with. I highly recommend this book to anyone in the youth ministry field at any point in their career. All will find useful insights here."

—Nina Jonson, director of children and youth ministry, Plymouth Congregational Church, Minneapolis, MN

YOUTH MINISTRY AS PEACE EDUCATION

YOUTH MINISTRY AS PEACE EDUCATION

Overcoming Silence, Transforming Violence

ELIZABETH W. CORRIE

FORTRESS PRESS

MINNEAPOLIS

YOUTH MINISTRY AS PEACE EDUCATION
Overcoming Silence, Transforming Violence

Copyright © 2021 Fortress Press, an imprint of 1517 Media. All rights reserved. Except for brief quotations in critical articles and reviews, no part of this book may be reproduced in any manner without prior written permission from the publisher. Email copyright@1517.media or write to Permissions, Fortress Press, Box 1209, Minneapolis, MN 55440-1209.

All Scripture quotations, unless otherwise indicated, are from the COMMON ENGLISH BIBLE. © Copyright 2011 COMMON ENGLISH BIBLE. All rights reserved. Used by permission. (www.CommonEnglishBible.com).

Scripture quotations marked (NRSV) are from the New Revised Standard Version Bible © 1989 Division of Christian Education of the National Council of the Churches of Christ in the United States of America. Used by permission.

Cover Design: Soupiset Design

Print ISBN: 978-1-5064-6945-4
eBook ISBN: 978-1-5064-6947-8

For
Rachel Ailene Corrie
April 10, 1979–March 16, 2003
Activist and Artist
Cousin and Friend

CONTENTS

Acknowledgments — ix

1. Shaping Images — 1
2. Building Community Democratically — 21
3. Learning Theology Deliberatively — 47
4. Reading the Bible Cacophonously — 69
5. Doing Mission Intersectionally — 91
6. Practicing Worship Prophetically — 117
7. Acting in the World Nonviolently — 145

Conclusion: Images That Shape Our Work — 173

Notes — 179

Selected Bibliography — 195

ACKNOWLEDGMENTS

This project was a labor of love. It is first and foremost an expression of love for young people and the people who journey with them. It is also an expression of love for the many colleagues and institutions that have nurtured my ideas and encouraged me to write them down. The conclusion of this book pays tribute to the former. The following pages pay tribute to the latter.

I am grateful for the support of the Louisville Institute, whose Sabbatical Grant for Researchers made it possible for me to take a full year's leave from my teaching and administrative duties to focus on research for the first time in my career and whose winter seminar connected me with other colleagues with whom to talk through my writing puzzles. Candler School of Theology, a place at which I arrived in 1993 as a master's student and now find myself privileged enough to serve as a faculty member, has consistently supported my growth as a scholar and teacher. Its Teaching and Research Fund underwrote editorial services to help me stay on track, and Jan Love, Mary Lee Hardin Willard Dean of Candler, and Jonathan Strom, senior associate dean of faculty and academic affairs at Candler, not only encouraged me but actively ensured that I could take this time for focused research. Emory University's Center for Faculty Development and Excellence also provided financial support for editorial services and project development.

Ulrike Guthrie, my editorial and pastoral support, not only helped me write better but guided me through the process of finding the right publisher. She led me to Beth Gaede, my editor at Fortress Press, who saw the importance of writing for an audience who cares about young people, an audience sometimes underserved as much as the youth themselves. Jennifer Ayres, Arun Jones, Kyle

Lambelet, and Lauren Calvin Cooke each took time to read drafts of chapters, providing me with critical feedback out of their own fields of expertise. Gregory Ellison II and Elizabeth Bounds served as peer reviewers, providing me sage advice I followed to great effect.

Early formations of my ideas were tested out within a "Think Tank on Peace Education," supported by the Lilly Youth Theology Network, which fostered conversations with Jeffrey Kaster, Russell Haitch, Andy Brubacher Kaethler, Jessica Joustra, Michael Tischel, Alaina Kleinbeck, Craig Gould, and Rachelle Green, each of whom shared with me the riches of their particular theological traditions, as well as our shared joy in teaching and learning with young people.

As a way to hold myself accountable to the young people about whom I was writing, I formed the Conclave, a group of youth and youth workers who agreed to read drafts and answer seemingly random questions as I tested my thoughts against their realities. In particular, I would like to thank Eric Rucker, Carmen Cunningham, C. J. Lord, Maria Caruso, Natalie Faria-Campbell, Haley Andreades Vermeer, Nina Jonson, Ellen Green, Jess Cusick, Elijah Shoaf, Durham Harris, Kim Jackson, Fiona Findlay, Kristian Canler, and Candice Austin Winn.

Without the Youth Theological Initiative (YTI), I would not have discovered my joy of working with young people, nor the wonder of God's ways in the midst of community. Thank you to Charles Foster for contributing so much to establishing and sustaining YTI over nearly three decades and for mentoring me as both a teacher and a researcher. Thank you to Don Richter for hiring me that first time in 1996. Thank you to Jill Weaver for receiving with loving arms a program that has been both mother and child to me. And thank you to all the young people—YTI staff and scholars—who allowed me into their lives and shared with me their hopes, challenges, and prophetic calls to action.

And finally, thank you to my family, Steve, Joan, and Cathleen, each of whom has loved me into the person I have become. And to Hazem, who loves me as the person I am.

Chapter One
SHAPING IMAGES

What's the common denominator among the hit Broadway musical *Hamilton*, the Gen X cult film *Dazed and Confused*, and the award-winning young adult novel *The Hate U Give*? Each depicts a particular image of young people. In each, the young characters explore their vocation, what purpose their lives serve in the world. Each work reveals something about the history of young people in North America. And each raises critical questions for those of us who love young people, particularly those of us who believe that the Christian faith has something life-giving worth sharing with these young people.

YOUNG, SCRAPPY, HUNGRY: A FORGOTTEN IMAGE OF YOUNG PEOPLE

Lin-Manuel Miranda's globally renowned musical *Hamilton* (2015) is as revolutionary as the historical moment it seeks to portray. It reminds those in the audience who still cling to an idea of American exceptionalism that the outcome of the Revolutionary War was by no means ensured, that someone had to persuade the former colonists of the new concepts of a democratic republic, and that those colonists made shameful compromises regarding slavery. The way that Miranda flips the script of America's founding myth challenges and inspires those in the audience who hold out hope that the injustices of racism and classism can still be transformed. Miranda refracts the script through the lens of "another immigrant coming up from the bottom" who hangs around with "a bunch of revolutionary manumission abolitionists"[1] and tells this story through the media of hip-hop and performers of color. It evokes dangerous memories of how inextricably race, class, gender, and immigrant status have always shaped—and *still* shape—the United States.

Less obviously, *Hamilton* evokes a dangerous memory[2] about young people.

Alexander Hamilton arrives in New York at age nineteen, eager to be part of the revolution that is rumored to be on the horizon. He introduces himself to Aaron Burr, the man who would become Hamilton's political rival and eventually kill him in a duel in 1804. Burr invites Hamilton to join him for a drink in a tavern, where we meet Hercules Mulligan, John Laurens, and the Marquis de Lafayette, all advocates for independence from the British Crown and all men who would later serve in roles critical to the success of the war as spies and soldiers. Confidently arriving on the scene, Hamilton declares himself "young, scrappy, and hungry," just like the new nation he wants to help create.

By the end of the song, Laurens, Lafayette, and Mulligan have joined Hamilton's chorus, all singing that they're "young, scrappy, and hungry" and will "rise up" to "take a shot" at winning independence. All of these men became close friends of Hamilton. All of these men were indeed scrappy fighters and hungry to change the world and contribute to the start of a new country—and they did so by becoming critical players in the Revolutionary War.

All of these men were also *young*. By 1776, Mulligan was the oldest of the bunch at age thirty-six, with Hamilton and Laurens twenty-one, Burr twenty, and Lafayette the youngest at eighteen.[3]

The "dangerous memory" that Miranda's *Hamilton* evokes for those of us who love youth is the fact that our country was not so much founded by "fathers" as by young people: *young people once did things with their lives that mattered, at the time they were doing them, and they did them for their communities and families as well as themselves.*

A MINOR, INSIGNIFICANT PREAMBLE TO SOMETHING ELSE: THE MODERN AMERICAN TEENAGER

The 1993 film *Dazed and Confused* became an instant cult hit among Gen Xers, with its quotable lines and an image of adolescence recognizable to young adults (like myself), who embraced with requisite irony the purposelessness that director Richard Linklater explored in his prior film *Slacker* and brought to comedic success in *Dazed and Confused*. Set in 1976 in Austin, Texas, *Dazed and Confused* takes us to a historical time and place entirely different from Hamilton's New York and portrays a very different image of young people.

The film begins on the last day of school. Teachers and students alike are watching the clock, waiting for the final bell and the freedom of summer to arrive. As the minutes tick by, we see several different cliques—football players, burnouts, popular girls, and nerds—discuss the plan for this first night of freedom. Unsurprisingly, the plan is a party at Pickford's house because his parents are going out of town for the weekend. However, once Pickford's parents get wind of the plan, they forego their trip and force their son to cancel the party. In the days before cell phones and group texts, it takes most of the night for the teenagers to discover that the party has been busted and to come up with an alternative plan. Meanwhile, they are in limbo—driving around the city looking for others, hanging around the arcade waiting for something else to happen, jumping in and out of each other's cars to share gossip or smoke pot, and diverting themselves with acts of delinquency, from throwing trash cans at mailboxes to stealing lawn statues and painting the statues' faces like members of the band KISS. The kids are bored. They're waiting for something to happen.

The movie does not have much of a plot, which is exactly the point. But there are two scenes that encapsulate this tale of teenagers. In the first scene, we find the nerdy clique—Cynthia, Mike, and Tony—aimlessly driving around the town. The pointlessness of the evening inspires reflection on a broader pointlessness:

Cynthia: God, don't you ever feel like everything we do and everything we've been taught is just to service the future?
Tony: Yeah I know, like it's all . . . preparation.
Cynthia: Right. But what are we preparing ourselves for?
Mike: Death.
Tony: Life of the party.
Mike: It's true.
Cynthia: You know, but that's valid because if we're all gonna die anyway, shouldn't we be enjoying ourselves now? You know, I'd like to quit thinking of the present, like right now, as some minor insignificant preamble to something else.[4]

Such insight resembles the wisdom of Ecclesiastes, who observed that "everything is pointless, a chasing after wind" (Eccl 1:14). The time spent preparing for a future adulthood is, for Cynthia and her peers, pointless.

In another scene, a handful of students, mostly from the football team, end up sitting on the school football field, sharing a joint and talking about their hatred of the rules that the school imposes on them. Chided for complaining, because as star quarterback he is a "king" of the school, Randall "Pink" Floyd declares, "Well, look, all I'm saying is that if I ever start referring to these as the best years of my life, remind me to kill myself." As he walks away from the group in frustration, Pink stares up at the stars while the camera pans around him in slow motion, signaling the climax. In the background, we hear the central message of the film, articulated by Pink's teammate Don: "Well, all I'm saying is that I want to look back and say that I did it the best I could while I was stuck in this place. Had as much fun as I could while I was stuck in this place. Played as hard as I could while I was stuck in this place." The teenagers we see here are (often literally) spinning their wheels and aware that their lives to this moment have been pointless. The best they can hope for is to have as much fun as they can while they are stuck in high school, waiting to become "real" adults.

MY VOICE IS MY WEAPON: IMAGES OF YOUTH IN THE TWENTY-FIRST CENTURY

Angie Thomas's debut young adult novel *The Hate U Give* (2017) tells the story of sixteen-year-old Starr Carter, a Black teenager who lives in an underserved, gang-dominated neighborhood called Garden Heights. Her father, formerly incarcerated, now runs the local grocery store, and her mother works as a nurse in the Garden Heights clinic. The parents are committed to the neighborhood from which they came but also want to see a better life for their children, and so Starr, like her other siblings, attends Williamson Prep, a private, almost entirely white school. She lives in two different worlds and, not unlike many young people, has two different identities: there's "Williamson Starr," the "exceptional Black person" who doesn't talk "ghetto" and doesn't threaten white, middle-class sensibilities, and then there's "Garden Heights Starr," who works in her father's grocery store and hangs out with her friend Kenya, whose father is the gang leader of the Garden Heights King Lords.

These two carefully segregated identities crash into each other when Starr witnesses the shooting death of her childhood friend Khalil in a clear example of police brutality. As Khalil's death becomes a national news story, one that portrays him as a gang member and implies he deserved his fate, Starr wrestles with whether and how to speak out for justice for her friend. Starr states, "I always said that if I saw it happen to somebody, I would have the loudest voice, making sure the world knew what went down. Now I am that person, and I'm too afraid to speak."[5]

But as the story progresses, Starr *does* speak. She agrees to give an interview on a local television show and to testify to a grand jury. Her parents and her lawyer tell her she is "brave," but she rejects the label. In Starr's mind, "Brave peoples' legs don't shake. Brave people don't feel like puking. Brave people sure don't have to remind themselves how to breathe if they think about that night too hard." Her mother helps Starr understand that bravery "doesn't mean you're not scared," but rather, "it means you go on even though you're scared. And you're doing that." With this encouragement, Starr decides to "straighten up and allow the tiny brave part of me to speak." By the end of the book, Starr allows that tiny brave part to speak from a megaphone as she stands on top of a police car in the middle of a riot protesting the acquittal of the police officer who killed her friend. She becomes an activist, committed to fighting for justice not only for Khalil but also for all the young men and women of color whose lives have been cut short by racism and police brutality. As she realizes it is her turn to join the fight, she promises "never [to] give up" and "never [to] be quiet."[6]

The Hate U Give is a coming of age novel for the Black Lives Matter era. It tells a tale of teenagers wrestling with racism and poverty, wrestling with life and death, and learning how to advocate nonviolently for justice. Starr declares, "This is how I fight, with my voice."[7]

But it also tells a tale of adults who love their young people, and it tells a tale about *faith*. In her house, "Black Jesus hangs from the cross in a painting on the hallway wall," and on the wall of the Garden Heights clinic in which her mother works, "Black Jesus greets us from a mural.... His arms stretch the width of the wall.... Big letters remind us that *Jesus Loves You*." While Starr's mother is more traditionally Christian, Starr's father "believes in Black Jesus but follows the Black Panther's Ten-Point Program more than the Ten Commandments." Even so, Starr's father regularly leads the entire family in prayer to "Black Jesus," and Starr's mother takes her and her brothers to church weekly. Starr's early memory of Khalil, in fact, is sharing her first kiss with him during vacation Bible school at Christ Temple Church. Starr has been raised going to church and in a family that takes faith seriously. And this is not incidental to her evolution into an activist. When Starr "wants to crawl up in a corner and act as if none of this ever happened," she realizes that "all those people outside are praying for me. My parents are watching me.

Khalil needs me."[8] Within the context of a supportive community of faith and a family that affirms her bravery, Starr learns how to fight for change using her "weapon"—her voice.

QUERYING IMAGES OF YOUTH

These cultural artifacts paint three distinct images of being young in North America. Hamilton and his friends are "just like [their] country ... young, scrappy, and hungry," ready to get out there and fight for independence and a new experiment in self-government. Despite their age, they are not waiting. Something important needs to be done, and Hamilton and his friends see their own identities, their own life paths, mapped out in responding to this historical moment. Their sense of vocation—what they are called to be doing with their lives—is clear and urgent. They are not throwing away their shot. They are the young Americans produced by the revolutionary ideas of the day.

In *Dazed and Confused*, however, we see a group of teenagers, a few years younger but quite close in age to Hamilton and his friends, with nothing to do. They have a vague sense that they are supposed to be preparing for adulthood but know they are not yet considered to be adults. Nothing they do really matters, except in service to the future, and as Pink states clearly, this time period is so small and meaningless that if they discovered that their high school years really were the best years of their lives, theirs would not be lives worth living. No one is calling them to do anything except bide their time while they are "stuck in this place" and keep hoping their future will be better than their present. They are passive. They are domesticated.[9] They are the teenagers produced by the idea of adolescence.

In *The Hate U Give*, we see a teenager who finds her way out of this domestication by resisting the criminalization of her friend. Khalil and Starr are the disposable youth produced by classism and racism. But Starr learns to defy this image imposed on her and her friends. All of the conversations about justice and oppression she has had with her parents, all the love of her family and friends, all the mentoring of the activists she encounters—all of this positions her to respond to the historical moment that is calling her to become a public advocate for justice. She is sixteen, and her clear-eyed understanding of right and wrong, unclouded by the many compromises and defeats that often prevent adults from speaking out, makes her a prophet. Like the biblical prophet Jeremiah, she starts out afraid that she does not know what to say, as she is only a child. But she discovers that words flow when the moment of truth comes. While Starr does not attribute this to God touching her mouth, as with Jeremiah, Black Jesus had something to do with giving Starr the courage to pick up that megaphone. Standing on top of a car, shouting to the crowds around her, Starr overcomes the silencing of young voices. This sets her on a path to transform the violence of racism, classism, and sexism around her.

These three distinct cultural images of youth raise the critical questions that undergird this book. Between the founding of the United States and our current moment, the role of young people in shaping their communities and their own lives has changed drastically. What happened? How have our views of young people changed? How have these changes shaped the institutions we have created for them, including churches, schools, government, and workplaces? How have these changes shaped the sense of vocation, identity, and meaning that young people have developed (or failed to develop)? What role can Christianity play in raising up young prophets? Does it require us to shift our image of who Jesus is? Does it require us to shift our image of what youth ministry is? Can parents, pastors, and activists work with young people to equip them to take their turn in the struggle for justice and true peace so that the violence and silence young people live *will* change one day, as Starr insists?

TWO SHAPING IMAGES OF TEENAGERS

When I ask youth workers and young people what stereotypes they see perpetuated about young people, they give me very specific and consistent examples. They overhear adults discussing young people as primarily interested in getting drunk or high or vaping. They are subjected to punitive dress codes that tell them that their bodies and clothing are too "distracting" (i.e., sexualized, referring primarily to girls) or too "disrespectful" (i.e., criminalized, referring to boys, particularly boys of color). They are followed around in stores because clerks assume they have come to steal. When they do something kind or polite, they are met with surprise because it is assumed they are too selfish or disrespectful to care for others. They are not allowed to take on leadership roles because they are seen as lazy, irresponsible, uncommitted, or only doing things to put on their college résumés. They are mocked for using their phones and assumed to be concerned only with social media, texting, and games. They are emotionally fragile "snowflakes" who can't take criticism. They don't care about the world around them, only about cultivating their social media image.

Their experiences signal the impact of two root images of youth that are dominant in North American culture: (1) *the incomplete adult* and (2) *the precocious delinquent*.[10] The incomplete adult is the image of Pink, Don, and the kids sitting on the football field in *Dazed and Confused*: lazy, spoiled, immature, undisciplined, selfish, irresponsible, vain, sheltered. Adults assume their lives are easy because they have been protected from adult responsibilities and the world of adult work, and so they dismiss their grievances as unjustified. Adults assume they can't trust these young people with meaningful work or leadership roles in the church, schools, or society. Marketers, however, value young peoples' enormous access to and influence over discretionary spending, and so it is as consumers that they are most affirmed.[11] Their job is to become economically productive adults—and *then* (maybe) we'll listen to them. Until then, they are to keep shopping but remain silent.

The precocious delinquent is the image pinned on Khalil in *The Hate U Give*: violent, sexually active, doing drugs, smoking, drinking, having children out of wedlock—*thug*. Adults see them as threatening because they dare to engage in adult activities, because they cannot or will not conform to white, middle-class behaviors, and so they must be controlled, contained, or eliminated. Although they may deny it when confronted directly, many adults don't believe these youth will ever engage in meaningful work or leadership roles in the church, schools, or society. Their job is to become submissive adults, and *then* (maybe) we'll let them live their lives—if they make it to adulthood. Until then, they are to accept the violence of alienation, harassment, incarceration, and extrajudicial killing.

Incomplete adults; precocious delinquents. I've drawn these two images starkly, but they suffuse adult attitudes toward youth in varying degrees of subtlety. And they represent two parallel yet interrelated images of youth in the United States: the image of white, middle-class youth as consumers and the image of working-class, immigrant, and Black and Brown youth as criminals. These images have historical roots.

Adolescence and the Rise of the Incomplete Adult

The publication in 1904 of G. Stanley Hall's two-volume tome *Adolescence: Its Psychology and Its Relations to Physiology, Anthropology, Sociology, Sex, Crime, Religion and Education* is often cited as the true beginning of the social construct known as the modern adolescent.[12] Hall was the first to designate adolescence as a distinct life phase, in between childhood and adulthood. Joseph Kett explains that for Hall, adolescence was "a new birth, a wiping clean of the slate of childhood," a time marked by "dualisms which disrupted the harmony of children; hyperactivity and inertia, social sensibility and self-absorption, lofty intuitions and childish folly," and which demanded a prolonged period in which "religious enthusiasm, idealism, altruism, moodiness, and inertia" could have free play and be expended fully "before safe passage to maturity was assured."[13]

This special time around puberty and into the early twenties was a time that Hall believed needed to be protected from "precocity"—from taking on adult roles and responsibilities too early. It was also, in Hall's view, a time of "storm and stress," in which young people were expected, as a natural process, to go through a season of turmoil. The image of moody, self-absorbed youth who need to be protected from themselves was born.

Hall's argument for a separate space for young people to move safely through the stage of adolescence before becoming adults became fused with economic and social drivers to extend the period of schooling, and by the end of World War II, the high school became the quintessential site for the adolescent experience. Between 1910 and 1940, high school enrollment skyrocketed, from 18 to 73 percent; by the 1950s and 1960s, nearly all young people and their families were involved.[14] The dominance of the high school had two important implications for how we view young people. First, it turned individual young people into a highly visible, distinct group—teenagers—about which we could now categorize, generalize, and organize. The social category of "teenager," a herd-like group to be managed rather than a set of individuals with whom to develop relationships, was born.[15]

Second, pulled away from their families and placed under the influence of teachers, administrators, and peers, young people used that time and space to develop their own youth culture, distinct from, and sometimes in conflict with, their parents' culture and authority. Teenagers and parents spent less and less time with each other, and immersed in a separate school culture, teenagers lost connections with the cultural past of their families.[16] The "generation gap," now assumed to be an inevitable facet of American culture, had its roots in the invention of the high school.

Hall receives much criticism for creating an image of youth that discounts their abilities as growing adults and sets them up for frustration as they are forced "for their own good" to stay away from adult responsibilities.[17] More recently, he has also come under fire for basing his theory of adolescence on ideas that were, at their core, racist, colonialist, and heterosexist. Hall based his understanding of adolescence on "recapitulation theory," a biological theory postulating that child development retraced the evolution of the human race. Just as young children discover the use of tools like prehistoric humans did, so adolescents went through a period of migration and upheaval, much like hunter-gatherers. Nancy Lesko points out that recapitulation theory specifically placed *white men* as the benchmark for development. It was a theory that not only compared children to "primitives" but also compared Indigenous people and Blacks to children and ranked other races and cultures along a Great Chain of Being based on European culture as the pinnacle. Adolescence became a fixation for many social reformers because it was at this point that children "leaped to a developed, superior, Western selfhood or remained arrested in a savage state." Consequently, adolescence became a "technology of 'civilization' and progress and of white, male, bourgeois supremacy."[18]

The incomplete adult image, rooted in Hall's theory, domesticates, disenfranchises, and silences young people. Our image of teenagers as naturally in turmoil is inextricably linked with our insistence that we can dismiss their grievances and viewpoints as irrational and control their movements and experiences "for their own good." Moreover, our image of teenagers as unevolved, incomplete adults is inextricably linked with race, class, and gender. If the goal of adolescence is to come out on the other side a white, male, bourgeois citizen, only a segment of young people in America can ever fully attain adulthood—and citizenship. The silencing of young voices helps ensure the ongoing silencing of the voices of people of color, LGBTQIA+ people, Indigenous people, working-class people, and women.

Superpredators and the Rise of the Precocious Delinquent

The Victorian-era "cult of domesticity" describes a time in which the wealthier white classes of the nineteenth century turned inward to nurture their young. This term obscures the fact that they were also trying to "protect" their children—from immigrants, Blacks, and poor children on the streets of the cities. The Irish potato famine of 1845–49 was, according to Thomas Hine, "a watershed in American life, and an end to republican ideals of social equality or industrial reform."[19] The members of this new immigrant labor source were in many places considered subhuman, and the sheer number of them flooding the eastern cities and mills created a fear of "dangerous classes" who were "given to drunkenness and crime, producing too many children, and adhering to a superstitious religion that retarded their progress." The "gangs of New York," made up of immigrant children and the children of poor native-born parents whose livelihoods were threatened by these immigrants, became a focus of public concern over juvenile delinquency.[20] Charles Loring Brace founded the New York Children's Aid Society in 1853 to save homeless and abandoned children on the city streets by giving them a family experience he presumed poor and immigrant families were incapable of providing. His "orphan trains" sent such youth (whether they were orphans or not) to live with rural families out west and is—revealingly—the model upon which our current foster care system is based.[21]

Just as the American high school gained popularity, the juvenile justice system arrived as its complement. Established with the first juvenile court in 1899 in Cook County, Illinois, this parallel justice system was based on the doctrine of *parens patriae*, the idea that the state as surrogate parent could intervene to protect young people from themselves and from their negligent families. However, pulling youth into a system of supervision meant to *prevent criminal behavior* quickly became a mechanism for recasting youthful actions *as criminal*. While many of the cases before the court were for stealing and "disorderly conduct," youth also came before the court charged with "incorrigibility," a term coined as a catchall for behaviors that were, while annoying, not illegal when practiced by adults—"'loitering about the streets and using vulgar language,' 'refusing either to go to work or to school, roaming the street late at night,' 'keeping bad company, refusing to obey parents, and staying away from home.'"[22] Youthful behaviors such as skipping school, hanging out with friends in public, and defying adults "gave authorities excuses to round up and put away virtually any young people—especially those of the lower classes."[23] Bourgeois reformers wanted to save children from a life of neglect and crime, but their reforms set up the conditions for the criminalization of young people and the penalization of families unable or unwilling to raise their children according to middle-class standards.[24]

By the 1990s, panic about young people hit an all-time high, and the image of the precocious delinquent morphed into something more sinister. In 1995, criminologist John J. DiIulio predicted a wave of youth crime that would hit the streets by 2010. In an article in the *Weekly Standard*, DiIulio conjured the image of "tens of thousands of severely morally impoverished juvenile super-predators" who were "perfectly capable of committing the most heinous acts of physical violence for the most trivial reasons." To make sure that the suburban white families got the message, he added, "While the trouble will be greatest in black inner-city neighborhoods, other places are also certain to have burgeoning youth-crime problems that will spill over into upscale central-city districts, inner-ring suburbs, and even the rural heartland."[25] The menace was just around the corner, and media reports around this time framed children growing into teenagers as a "plague," a "teenage time bomb," a "tsunami," and an "invasion."[26] Precocious delinquents became more than a problem for reformers to address: they became a disease, a natural disaster, an act of war—criminals that must be contained, violently if necessary.

Images Matter

In 1993, at the same time American society was starting to see young people as "superpredators," youth worker Kirk Astroth coined the term *ephebiphobia*, the fear and loathing of young people. He noted, "Young people today are typically portrayed as some aberrant and pariah class suffering its own distinct 'epidemics' that are different from behavior of previous generations and bear no relationship to adult patterns of behavior."[27] Perceptively, Astroth could see the danger in the images adults projected onto young people: our fear *for* young people as a distinct group that must be set apart to protect them from growing up too fast easily morphs into a fear *of* young people as the bearers of our societal dysfunctions, including racism, classism, and a disvaluing of people who do not fit into a consumer capitalistic system in the roles given to them. Our claims to care about young people "as our future" all too often conceal our discomfort with young people in the present—particularly if they dare to claim their individuality or agency.

When adults see young people as lazy, irresponsible, stupid, self-centered, spoiled, vain, fragile, or shallow, we dismiss them when they try to tell us about the very real harm they are experiencing and witnessing. We assume they cannot possibly be taken seriously, because they are too sheltered to know about the "real world." They are too mentally unstable or emotionally sensitive and cannot be trusted to judge whether something is "really" racist or sexist or homophobic or simply unjust. They cannot be activists, because they are not committed enough to stay engaged, need to focus on school, and anyway don't really care about anyone but themselves. Because we have domesticated young people, keeping them warehoused in schools and entertained with consumer culture, we are unable and unwilling to hear their voices. This book seeks to help adult advocates equip youth to speak in order to overcome this silencing.

When adults see young people as druggies, delinquents, or thugs, we miss the underlying economic, political, legal, and social dynamics that enmesh them in cycles of neglect, suspicion, containment, and disposability. Their protests, no matter how peaceful, are framed as dangerous, and when their frustrations boil over into rioting, we clamp down even harder and self-righteously chide them for bringing death and destruction on themselves. We turn schools into detention centers and send youth to adult prison. We cut funding for education, health services, and food assistance.

We shoot them in the streets. Because we have criminalized young people, keeping them warehoused in detention centers or ghettos, we have sanctioned unconscionable harm on them and encouraged them to visit this harm on themselves and others. This book seeks to help adult advocates teach skills for peace building and justice seeking that can transform this violence into peace with justice.

RESHAPING OUR IMAGES

The resources and insights offered in this book have evolved over twenty-five years of working with young people through the Youth Theological Initiative (YTI), a residential program for high school youth hosted by Candler School of Theology, Emory University, in Atlanta, Georgia. This program has gathered hundreds of youth from around the world, across a wide range of racial, ethnic, denominational, theological, political, socioeconomic, gender, and cultural identities and experiences. Summer after summer, youth and adults have learned how to live together, building intentional communities marked by commitments to seeking justice, building peace, and connecting our faith to the needs of the world. YTI has revealed to me the lies of the incomplete adult and precocious delinquent images of youth, and the silencing and violence that these lies have wrought on young people. YTI has also revealed to me the amazing capabilities of young people, which they can put to use once adults learn how to affirm those capabilities, equip youth to use those capabilities more effectively, and then get out of their way so that they can lead *now*.

YTI has given me, along with all the staff and youth who have participated in it over the years, the opportunity to unmask and resist those harmful images of young people. This book invites us to engage in a process of weaning ourselves and our youth away from these disempowering and dangerous images. Youth are not lazy; they are disempowered by adults who dismiss them and refuse to let them lead, and they are bored with meaningless busywork. Youth are not predators; they are preyed upon by adults who use them for their own agendas or target them for being outside the acceptable class, race, immigrant, gender, or sexual identity. This book also invites us to reshape images of youth into more empowering ones. Youth are not consumers or criminals; they are citizens of their civic and faith communities. Youth are not the future; they are the present. Youth are not meant to accept injustice and violence passively; they are meant, like all of us, to work actively toward establishing God's *shalom*—peace, justice, and well-being—on earth as it is in heaven.

The resources and insights offered in this book also come from reading Scripture in conversation with biblical scholars and theologians. They come from scholars who have sought to illumine our sacred texts by uncovering the historical context of first-century Palestine, the editorial and literary efforts of New Testament writers, the influence of these texts on communities since they were written, and the role each reader plays in interpreting these texts, even today. These approaches to biblical interpretation are historical-critical, literary, cultural, feminist, womanist, liberationist, and postcolonial. They include wisdom from Jewish and Muslim scholars, as well as scholars from across the Christian family. This scholarship has revealed to me the distortions of Western images of Jesus that portray him as white and European more than as a Palestinian Jew, that focus on his death more than his life, that focus on a future otherworld more than the kin(g)dom[28] of God brought near, that suggest his teachings are impractical and idealistic rather than strategic and highly attuned to the context of people on the ground.

This book invites us to engage in a process of critically examining our assumed understandings of Jesus Christ and allow ourselves to be challenged by images that might at times trouble our most deeply held beliefs. Because the goal of this book is action, I have chosen to focus on what Jesus and his followers *do* more than what they *say*. By looking closely at several biblical stories, new images of Jesus will emerge. Jesus is a convener of community. A deliberator of difficult ideas. A scriptural debater.

A recovering colonizer. A practicing Jew. A nonviolent campaigner. Starr Carter's Jesus is Black, and Black liberationist and womanist scholars understand the power of moving away from oppressive images of Jesus toward images of Jesus that free us from the forces of violence and injustice. If Starr's image of Jesus contributes to her journey toward freedom, we must consider the images of Jesus contributing to ours and to those of our youth.

The resources and insights offered in this book also derive from my foray into theories and practices developed in fields outside of some traditional youth ministry and religious education sources. They come from practitioners and researchers engaged in service learning, civic engagement, deliberative democracy, Jewish education, nonviolence theory and strategy, and peace psychology. These sources have given us new tools for our toolboxes and offered us different ways to approach youth ministry. They remind us that teaching and mentoring young people is serious work, and they hold up new images for us as youth workers. We are not entertainers; we are organizers and equippers. We are not babysitters; we are fellow citizens and members of the body of Christ. We are not experts; we are colearners fumbling our way toward faithful discipleship. We refuse to perpetuate the silencing of youth. We refuse to perpetuate violence against and by youth.

If we want to reclaim the dangerous memory of "young, scrappy, and hungry" leaders and resist the domestication and criminalization of teenagers by working alongside youth to become peace builders and justice seekers, we must reshape youth ministry as peace education. The following chapters contribute to this effort by showing ways to integrate new tools and insights into the typical facets of congregational youth ministry: building community, learning theology, reading Scripture, going on mission and service trips, and engaging in worship, prayer, and spiritual practices. The final chapter suggests an additional facet of congregational youth ministry needed in order for young people to overcome silence and transform violence: preparing and planning for engaging the world nonviolently.

We have multiple images of youth and youth ministers before us, some dangerous in the ways they justify oppression, some dangerous in the ways they threaten those forces that benefit from oppression. The most dangerous image of all is the one God gave us: *imago Dei*. Young people are not the projections we place on them: they are marvelously set apart as God's creation. If we truly believe that each and every young person is formed in the image of God, then we must engage in ministry that affirms and reveals that image in our young people, for themselves as well as for a world that so desperately needs them—now.

Chapter Two
BUILDING COMMUNITY DEMOCRATICALLY

"We can make decisions? Really?"[1]

Two sets of eyes stared skeptically back at Rachelle, former assistant director of the Youth Theological Initiative (YTI). The persons' raised eyebrows and crossed arms projected a defensive, almost protective posture. But something in their voices betrayed their disbelief. It was the soft, lyrical quality of hope that any ear who has ever yearned for its song could recognize . . . and she did. So she repeated her opening remarks: "You two have been selected as scholar[2] representatives to serve on the Governance Council for our community. You, in collaboration with myself and two other staff persons, will address any concerns, make needed changes, and handle any conflicts that arise. You were selected because you exhibit wisdom, a faithfulness to the goodness of this community, and the respect of your peers. All of us here have wisdom and God-given gifts to offer the community, and I am so glad to have you both on this council."

With these remarks, Rachelle welcomed two young people into YTI's Governance Council. She then welcomed the other two members of the council—one who is a teacher, the other, one of YTI's mentors, both adult members of the community living alongside the youth as part of our residential program. Finally, she gave a brief refresher about the purpose of the council and how the meeting would operate: "As you know, the Governance Council is the democratic governing body of the YTI community. I do not have a set agenda for this meeting. It is our time to hear and respond to God, our neighbors, and ourselves as we reflect on the state of our community—to see what is working well, to see what needs to be adjusted, and to address any concerns. So what should we talk about today?"

After a brief pause, the teacher in the group responded.

"I spoke with others in the community, and it seems that everyone is really tired. The schedule feels a bit overwhelming at times." The others agreed.

"Do you have any suggestions for what we should do? Should we make changes to the schedule, perhaps?"

"We can change the schedule?"

Rachelle smiled. "Yes, the Governance Council can propose to change the schedule. But it is not as simple as it sounds. We must think through the elements on the schedule, why they are there in the first place, and see what can be changed without compromising anything we feel is vital to our time together. If the community is in accord, the schedule changes."

"That's fantastic. Let's do it."

So they looked at the schedule, and after discussion and debate, they agreed on changes that they would present to the community later that day.

"Is there anything else we need to discuss?"

There was hesitation, then one of the scholars spoke up. "We need to talk about Riley."[3]

A collective head nodding ensued. Rachelle asked if anyone wanted to say more. Taking turns, everyone in the group had stories to share about Riley.

Riley was one of the students in the program who seemed to be having a hard time finding a place in the community. In their short time together, Riley had offended several students and had off-putting interactions with staff. Many people had already spoken to Riley about this behavior, but nothing had changed. The council spent the next hour talking about the dynamics of their community, reminding themselves of the type of community they wanted to be. Rachelle noted that although in times of conflict it is natural to want to revert to familiar models of punishment and discipline, the YTI community strives to respond with an ethic of love, especially in the face of conflict.

One of the scholars suggested that perhaps they were not doing their part as a community to get to know Riley better.

"We're the body of Christ, right? So Riley is part of Christ too."

The council agreed that there were things Riley needed to do. But it was clear to this scholar that there were also things the entire community needed to do. So they came up with a plan both to ask a trusted staff person to meet with Riley one-on-one and to ask Riley's peers to get to know Riley better—to practice love where it seemed the hardest. This scholar reminded the group what they had learned just that week about nonviolent communication[4] and holy listening[5] and urged them to think about what it means for their community to *be* the body of Christ.

With this democratic exchange, a small group of staff and scholars—adults and teenagers—practiced the art of faithful governance, theological reflection, and peace building for the YTI community. It embodied several aspects of what it means to build community with young people in ways that empower them to overcome the silencing of their voices and to transform the dynamics of coercion and violence that, even in contexts where the majority of the participants appear to be doing well, subtly cause alienation and harm to some of its members. It was a teaching moment: Rachelle used the democratic practice of a governance council to help the youth see that their voices mattered, and the discussion allowed the group to acknowledge a place where the community was hurting and connect their attempts to transform the situation into a core insight of Christian theology: the church as the body of Christ, an interconnected community made up of different members with different gifts—and different challenges. The Governance Council is just one example of doing youth ministry in a way that equips young people to overcome our larger culture's undemocratic silencing of their voices and transform the violent exclusion and blaming of young people.

BUILDING A DEMOCRATIC COMMUNITY:
JESUS AND A YOUTH FEED FIVE THOUSAND

The miracle of Jesus feeding a mass of people is the one miracle story that appears in all four gospels, which tells us something about how central this story was for the early Christians. John, however, seems to be up to something unique in his telling of the story, and it is worth looking closely at how he does it. In feeding the five thousand with the barley loaves and fish of a young person, Jesus teaches us something about building community with young people.

The overall movement of the story in John 6:1–15 is familiar to us. A crowd gathers in a place away from town. Jesus and the disciples discuss the problem of feeding this crowd. They invite the people to sit down, Jesus blesses a small amount of food, and it is distributed to the people. They eat and are satisfied, and far more food is gathered up than was present at the beginning.

What often escapes our attention are some of the details John includes. First, unlike in the case of the crowds in Matthew, Mark, and Luke, the crowd in John's version is not necessarily hungry. In John 6:2, John states that the crowd followed Jesus because "they had seen the miraculous signs he had done among the sick," but he does not say that they have been there a long time and that the time was getting late, as in the other accounts, and he does not say—nor does Jesus or the disciples—that the people are hungry. The people have followed Jesus for another reason; they do not necessarily expect Jesus to feed them.

Second, although all of the other accounts mention that the crowd sits down on the grass, John makes a point of saying that there was "plenty of grass" on which everyone could sit (John 6:10). Considering the image of abundance that the food will come to signify in this story, the suggestion that the space was also abundant seems important to note.

Third, obviously, is the inclusion of a young person in the story. While in the other accounts the five loaves and two fish seem to be among the disciples' collective possessions, in John, their source is very specific: a young person who happened to be nearby and whom Andrew had noticed.

Fourth, while all of the gospels mention that there are baskets of leftover fragments, only John has Jesus state why these fragments were gathered up: "so that nothing will be wasted" (John 6:12). While of course the gathering up of the leftovers into twelve baskets demonstrates the abundance of food that came out of the originally small amount, the leftovers seem to have a greater significance in John's telling.

Fifth, while in all the other accounts the story ends with the report of the leftovers, John tells how the people responded. In John 6:14–15, the people proclaim that Jesus is a "prophet who is coming into the world," and Jesus realizes that "they were about to come and force him to be their king," prompting him to flee to the mountain for solitude. Later, the crowd finds Jesus on the other side of the lake and asks him to give them another sign (v. 30), as well as to provide them with the bread of God "all the time" (v. 34).

Each of these details matters as we imagine what is happening in this story and what it might tell us about building community. One insight is that the miracle of the feeding, as told by John at least, is not primarily about satisfying hunger but about *building community through the sharing of food*. Jesus demonstrates what it takes to build community: a host willing to bring people together and attend to the wisdom at the heart of every church potluck, youth pizza party, family dinner, and holiday feast—sharing food brings people closer together. Words like *companion* and *accompany* share the Latin root of *pan*, "bread," and literally mean people who break bread with each other. When people sit down and eat together, they do more than eat. They talk, share stories, let down their defenses, and come to trust each other. In this story, Jesus plays the host; he invites people to sit down and become companions with each other by breaking bread together. This will become even more important later in the chapter when Jesus explains to this same group of people that *he* is the bread of life and that he will host everyone: "I won't send away anyone who comes to me" (John 6:37). He is the master of hospitality—all are welcome. All have a place at the table.

The abundance of grass also underscores the theme of hospitality. As any good host knows, *the physical space where people gather matters.* A dinner party that brings people together must occur in a space that is large enough for everyone to be able to see each other and yet also allow for smaller conversation groups to cluster so people can hear each other when they speak. That is why Jesus wants everyone to sit down. Mark and Luke specify that Jesus wanted the people to form groups as they sat down, and we can assume that in John some sort of subdivision happens here as well.

In this plentiful space of grass, we can imagine not only that people sat down but that they might have had enough space to stretch out, lean back, and eat in the leisurely banqueting style of that time. By sitting down, people could relax, but by being on the same level, they also could see each other better. They see and speak with each other rather than all facing Jesus. It is impossible not to imagine the members of the crowd talking with each other as they pass around the food. It is not difficult to imagine that as the food is passed around, people who had their own provisions with them pulled them out, offering them to each other. Imagine a sunny spring day, lounging in the grass, enjoying a picnic with people who have, like you, come to find out who this person is who has the power to heal. In my imagination, I combine the best church potluck with the best outdoor concert to catch a glimpse of what this might have been like. At least in this moment, the crowd is no longer an indistinguishable mass of followers but a group of individuals becoming a community. This suggests the insight that *we build community through a network of small groups supported by time and space for good conversation.*

Another insight from John's story is that *Jesus is showing us that if we are willing to include everyone and to bring their gifts from the margins to the center, we will have all we could want and abundance left over to share with others.* Unlike in the other gospels, in John, Jesus initiates the conversation about how to feed the crowd, and John makes clear that Jesus did this intentionally to "test" Philip, because "he already knew what he was going to do" (John 6:6). Jesus poses a problem to Philip and Andrew: "Where will we buy food to feed these people?" (6:5). Philip responds as most of us would: we can't buy food anywhere because we don't have the money to do it. He has calculated the need and determined that the problem is lack of funds. It can't be done. Andrew, however, notices a "youth" who has five barley loaves and two fish. He has at least begun the process of taking inventory of what they have already. Nonetheless, he gives up too, because even though he has noticed the important gift this young person has to give, he quickly determines that it is not enough and therefore dismisses the idea entirely. Both Philip and Andrew exemplify a mindset that must have been just as common then as it is today: focusing on what they don't have and can't do. Even with a young person standing right in front of them with something essential to contribute, they can only see the situation's deficiencies, not its possibilities.

Jesus, however, sees the possibilities, and he wants the disciples—and us—to see them too. Of course five loaves and two fish are not enough to feed five thousand people (more if we assume that John is only counting the adult men), but that was not what Jesus was asking. Where can they get the food? They'll find it together by building on what they already have. Whether we see the miracle as Jesus making the five loaves and two fish themselves into more food or we see it as a moment that inspires everyone who is sitting on the grass to check their own bags and add their own gifts to the mix, it is miraculous that a situation originally defined as a problem, a lack of resources, becomes the fulfillment of new possibility, a community that has found what it needs among its own people.

For us, John's most delightful insight is that this miracle happens when an adult—Andrew—notices a young person's gifts. While many translations refer to this young person as a lad or a boy, the

Greek here is gender neutral. We can imagine any young person within our community with gifts to share that are essential, not just for our particular youth ministry, but for the entire community. Jesus brings the gifts of the young person from the margin, where Andrew had dismissed them, into the center. Jesus takes that young person's gifts, gives thanks for them, and distributes them to the crowd, which then enjoys a community-building feast.

Not only this, but after all are satisfied, Jesus asks the disciples to gather up the leftovers into baskets "so that nothing will be wasted" (John 6:12). While the other gospels include the gathering up of leftovers, only John's version offers a reason. The leftovers are gathered up, not just to demonstrate the abundance created in this moment, but to be saved to be used elsewhere. Jesus wants this abundance to spill over, to feed everyone, to bring everyone into the circle.

John's Jesus repeatedly emphasizes his desire to be inclusive: he will not turn away or lose anyone the Father gives to him (John 6:37, 39; 17:12; 18:9). He has now given the disciples and the people food to share. Did he hope the people would take these leftovers back to their villages and families? Did he hope the disciples would each take their basket, go off into different directions, and continue sharing these gifts? Imagine how the miracle of the moment could have been spread further as people took those leftovers and gave them out to others, sharing the story of what happened as they did so, bringing more people into the circle.

Unfortunately, this is not what happened.

A final insight we can draw from John's version of this story is that *the habits of passivity and an unwillingness to be accountable to each other for making change are the biggest challenges we face in building transformative community.* While the other gospel accounts end with the image of leftovers in the baskets, John alone describes how the people react to the miracle. They proclaimed him a prophet. And just like Moses, whom the Israelites considered both prophet and king, they decided they wanted this prophet to be their king (John 6:14–15). Jesus intuits their desire and flees, leaving the disciples standing with the baskets and the people confused about what to do next. The disciples themselves decide to go back to Capernaum (one wonders what they did with the baskets of food), with Jesus catching up to them by walking on water. The people follow later in their own boats and catch up to Jesus on the other side of the lake. In a dialogue in which Jesus tries to explain that they should be looking for something more than earthly food—namely, him, the bread of life sent from heaven—the people demand an additional sign so that they can believe and ask Jesus to give them bread "all the time" (v. 34). They cannot seem to break away from conventional thinking: Jesus has done something powerful; therefore he needs to become a king, to rule over them in the same dynamic of domination of any earthly king. Jesus tells them that there is a different kind of bread, something eternally satisfying, and rather than making the choice to believe in Jesus, they ask Jesus to keep them dependent on a regular supply of food, like the manna the Israelites depended on while wandering in the desert with Moses. The people want Jesus to do all the work: rather than take from the experience of sitting on the grass a vision of how to build community with each other, of sharing their gifts and becoming mutually accountable to each other, the people want Jesus to be a conventional leader, making the decisions for them so they can remain passive, waiting for the next food delivery.

For John, the feeding of the five thousand story extends beyond the moment on the grass, going into the walking on water miracle and ending with the people following Jesus to the other side of the lake in order to press him into leading them in conventional terms. For this reason, John's miracle story teaches us something, not just about what we can do if we accept Jesus's invitation to imagine possibilities that go beyond our conventional thinking, but also about how hard it is to overcome that conventional thinking. The people want a king so that they do not have to be responsible for their own actions. They want to be fed, but they don't want to continue to feed each other. They've participated in a miracle—a young person's gifts came into the center from the margins and inspired them to sit down and become companions with each other—and yet they demand more signs, as though what they just experienced wasn't enough. The baskets of leftovers lie rotting on the shores of the lake. An opportunity for building a transformative community has been lost.

BUILDING DEMOCRATIC COMMUNITY THROUGH BELONGING AND ACCOUNTABILITY

In *Community: The Structure of Belonging*, Peter Block captures many of the insights revealed in John's depiction of the feeding of the five thousand, drawing them together into a theory and strategy for building transformative community—what I believe Jesus invited the crowd to do that day on the mountain. Block wants to do more than just help people solve problems; he wants to shift our very understanding of what community means and can do. He asks, "What is the means through which those of us who care about the whole community can create a future for ourselves that is not just an improvement, but one of a different nature from what we now have?"[6] For Block, the essential ingredient is a shared sense of *belonging*—the realization that each of us is a critical member of the community and is interdependent on all the other members. When we belong, we know that our voices and actions count, and because they count, we identify as part of the community and care about what happens to it. But more than this, when people belong to a community, they can transform the world around them in ways they might never have imagined. When people belong, they offer their gifts to the whole—whatever loaves and fish they have— and those gifts miraculously feed everyone.

Block's project is to describe the "structure" necessary to create a sense of belonging among people and move away from our current context, what he calls the "stuck community." The stuck community "markets fear, assigns fault, and worships self-interest." It clings to the past and believes "the future will be improved with new laws, more oversights, and stronger leadership." It idealizes the corporate model and places economic interests at the center. It looks to professionals to solve problems and sees itself in terms of what it lacks. It identifies scapegoats to avoid taking responsibility for making change itself. It fosters apathy and passivity, because its members do not believe they can contribute or that their contributions really make a difference. It "provides the argument for monarchy" rather than democracy, because it has no faith in its members to be able to improve their contexts without external resources and dependency on a strong leader.[7]

The crowd following Jesus was a stuck community. Rather than realizing the power they have in coming together with each other to share their gifts, the power of the Holy Spirit moving whenever two or three are gathered, the people wanted to make Jesus an earthly king who would rule over them and allow them to continue to be passive and unaccountable to each other. With Jesus as king, they could assign blame to all those who have oppressed them and cheer on their king as he smites them. They asked Jesus to give them the bread "all the time" (John 6:34) because they didn't want to feed each other and because they could not imagine a different kind of bread, a bread that sends them out into the world to change it rather than a bread that keeps them constantly dependent and passive. They followed Jesus to the mountain because they had seen that he could heal (6:2), but they did not recognize that the miracle of the feeding was also a healing miracle—the healing of broken community.

More than ever before, our broken communities need healing. Block's description captures well much of what is going on in the United States today, and it is not a stretch to describe most of our churches as stuck communities as well. It also helps us understand some of the challenges facing our youth and youth work. In chapter 1, I described images of young people as incomplete adults and precocious delinquents, images that represent a history of domestication and criminalization of young people, or *ephebiphobia*—the fear *of* and *for* young people that keeps us so invested in controlling and surveilling them and blaming them for society's ills. We fear that our young people are in danger and are dangerous, and this fear is big business—there are apps to keep tabs on their social media usage, expensive extracurricular activities to make sure every waking moment is occupied, or juvenile detention centers and for-profit prisons to keep the "worst" of them off the streets. We assign fault to them at every turn. They are leaving church and thus killing it; they are too shallow and uneducated and spoiled and thus making our country weak; they are too violent, too gullible, too fragile, too immoral to be worthy of political power. As adults, we project onto young people all that we most hate about ourselves—*our* ambivalence with church, *our* political apathy and division, *our* own violence, immorality, and fragility. And so, in our stuck mindset, we hire professionals (teachers, coaches, youth pastors, counselors, tutors) and pass new laws and create more rules (curfews, zero-tolerance policies, and high-stakes testing) to "fix" the problems with our young people rather than fostering a community of adults and young people making change together. We see young people as problems to be solved rather than as possibilities for a transformed future together.

As an antidote to the stuck community, Block envisions a community that restores our social fabric and so radically shifts our mindset to make possible a truly different future—a transformation. A core assumption in his project is that language and space matter. Block suggests that for humans to shift the way we live, we must shift the way we think; to do that, we must shift the way we talk and the way we gather. Rather than fixate on problems, we shift to see the possibilities. Rather than focus on fear and trying to figure out who is at fault, we shift to focus on abundance and generosity and try to figure out what gifts are among us. Rather than discuss how to impose more laws and oversight on others, we shift to discussions of freely chosen mutual accountability, the promises we make to each other. Rather than hire outside professionals to provide services to deal with our problems, we shift to inviting our neighbors to come together in voluntary associations. Rather than search for the one strong leader to take care of things for us, we shift to seeking out groups of citizens who work together to make things happen. Rather than talk about what we are entitled to—the services we've paid for or the benefits we expect from our designated leader—we shift to talking about our accountability to each other. Rather than act like consumers or clients, we start acting like citizens. For Block, "Restoration comes from the choice to value possibility and relatedness over problems, self-interest, and the rest of the stuck community's agenda. It hinges on accountability chosen by citizens and their willingness to connect with each other around promises they make to each other."[8] It is in becoming *citizens* who use our freedom and power to contribute to the common good that we restore the brokenness plaguing our society—and our churches.

In order to build democratic, transformative community with young people, in order to restore relationships among youth and adults, we can make some similar shifts in our thinking and in our language. Rather than seeing young people as problems—in danger or posing a danger—we choose to see first their possibilities. Rather than complaining about the size of our youth group or our youth ministry budget, we choose to believe that whoever shows up can build a community together that exceeds what we could have imagined. Rather than focusing on what we think young people need, we work to uncover, name, and cultivate the gifts they already have, encouraging them to share generously by establishing a culture in which they won't be shamed for doing so. Rather than creating a long list of rules that assume that young people must be coerced or bribed into participation in youth group, we scrap the rules and create a covenant with the youth that invites us all to be accountable to each other by choice. Rather than subtly pressuring youth to come to youth group or Sunday school because we need to bulk up our numbers, we issue true invitations, always communicating welcome but never suggesting guilt or judgment if they decline. Rather than taking on all the responsibility to lead young people, and rather than singling out the same handful of youth to do everything, we welcome every young person who shows up for our gatherings as fellow citizens essential to the work of the group. Rather than offering services to families, treating them as clients or consumers entitled to receive packaged events and experiences that we create for them, we work together to determine what we want to do and how we will do this together. Block's core question for community and Jesus's core question in the Gospel of John's account of the feeding of the five thousand should be the core question of our youth ministry: "What can we create together?"[9]

When we treat each other like citizens rather than like clients and service providers, problems and professional problem solvers, we stop instrumentalizing people, we stop building walls between each other, and we start belonging. The word *belong* has two meanings, Block emphasizes. In the first definition, the one that most easily comes to mind, "to belong" means "to be related to and a part of something . . . the experience of being at home in the broadest sense of the phrase." It is the opposite of feeling that "wherever I am, I would be better off somewhere else." Every youth worker, indeed every adult who loves young people, wants for their youth a place where they can feel at home and feel that they are better off for being in that place—this is the core of relational youth ministry. It is why we are distressed when they don't come or when they come but stay on their phones the whole time or when we see some of our youth being excluded or ignored. We want our youth to belong to our youth group. What Block's insights tell us is that the second definition of belonging is critical to making the other one happen. In the second definition, to belong means to be owned—something belongs to me. Block reminds us that "what I consider mine I will build and nurture."[10] In other words, if our youth belong to our youth group, they not only feel that they are loved by the group, but they also see it as *their* group, something whose direction and operation is determined by *them*. Most youth ministers work hard to make sure all of the young people in the group know they belong to a loving community. Do as many work hard to make sure all of the young people in the group know that this community belongs to, and is therefore dependent on, them?

PRACTICES THAT BUILD DEMOCRATIC COMMUNITY WITH YOUTH

Since 1993, YTI has been gathering a diverse group of young people into what we call "communities of commitment and accountability on behalf of the public good."[11] Young people across a wide range of theological perspectives, cultural backgrounds, and geographical origins choose to spend a portion of their summer vacations living together on Emory University's campus, building an intentional community with adult mentors, who also come from a diverse range of backgrounds and experiences. In our early years, the program lasted four weeks, but in recent years we have shortened the program to two weeks, acknowledging the many challenges young people have cramming all that is expected of them into an ever-shortening summer vacation. Though living together so intensively for four weeks taught us many lessons about the transformative possibilities of intentional community, we have also realized that these possibilities are still there in shorter blocks of time. If, as Block believes, "every time we gather becomes a model of the future we want to create,"[12] then all of our youth gatherings, whether a Sunday night fellowship gathering, a Wednesday morning Bible study, a weekend retreat, or a weeklong mission trip, can be an opportunity for us to build democratic, transformative community. It also means that, though YTI has wisdom to share based on gathering young people into community for an extended period of time, we believe this wisdom translates into any kind of gathering with youth. While an extended retreat makes it easier to step out of a stuck community and create a restorative one, a well-designed weekly gathering can, over time, embody an alternative future into being. If we pay attention to the structure of belonging, we can build community that overcomes the silence of youth disempowerment and transforms the violence of ephebiphobia. Though YTI's practices evolved separately from Block's methods, his strategy helps us understand how we were able to build a democratic, transformative community that fosters authentic belonging with our youth and welcomes the kind of exchanges with which I opened this chapter.

Choosing New Structures of Belonging: Planning for Community

Humans are social beings. We want to come together. But we can no longer leave this up to chance. Because we live in a culture dominated by values of individualism, self-interest, competition, and fear, whenever we gather people together, we have to work overtime to counteract the destructive forces that lead us into unhealthy, stuck communities. All of us—our young people, our adult volunteers, and we ourselves as youth workers—are burdened and deformed by these destructive forces, the ones that make us believe that our worth is only in our grades, salaries, or worship attendance numbers; the ones that make us believe that we need experts to tell us what to do and what to believe; the ones that make us believe that we cannot trust young people or ourselves to be the change we want to see. We have to remind ourselves regularly that we are free to choose to live differently. And before any young person walks into the room, we have to prepare ourselves, and the space, to make that choice visible.

The first choice we make is how we see ourselves as leaders. During YTI staff training, we spend a great deal of time talking about the importance of sharing power with young people. This is a difficult and nuanced approach and can create problems if not understood well. Sharing power is not the same as giving up power. We are not asking staff members to "let the kids walk all over them." We are not asking them to treat youth as they would their own friends, burdening young people with inappropriate sharing from their personal lives. We *are* inviting staff members to let go of some of the authoritarian models with which they grew up: teachers who bribed them with grades and special recognition or threatened them with punishment and public humiliation, pastors who told them what to believe or scolded them for not conforming to a specific set of behavioral standards, adults who punished them when they asked too many questions or resisted their agenda. The sweet spot is an approach to working with young people in which we listen to them, take their concerns and ideas seriously, and invite them into a process of building something new together. To get there takes practice, and we have to set up structures in order to make this easier to embody (more below). So in our very first conversations with all adults who interact with our youth, we articulate a vision of leadership in which we see ourselves as conveners of a community that seeks equality and accountability. We are not experts, gurus, babysitters, or playmates. We are conveners, and we are citizens.

The second choice we make is how to create hospitable spaces. For a residential community to grow, we need a common gathering space that is comfortable and has room for everyone. The furniture should be movable and soft, useful for lounging, for creating different small groups, for bringing the entire group together in a circle. This space, or another handy space, must also be large enough for everyone in the community to eat together well—that is, at tables, not sitting on the floor or balancing food on one's lap. In addition to this, we like to have several separate spaces. One is for engaging in arts and crafts, a place where music can be played softly while people work on projects and chat and where spills of paint or glitter are anticipated and cleaned up easily. Another is for prayer and meditation, set up with an altar, chairs facing each other for antiphonal prayer, places on the floor to sit comfortably for centering prayer and meditation, and icons, prayer beads, and prayer books available from a variety of Christian traditions so that each member of our community finds their own tradition represented and has a chance to explore the spiritual practices of other Christian traditions. We also need a quiet room or library, a place for introverts to take breaks from the bustle of the common room, to explore books, to chat quietly with a smaller group of people. Finally, we need access to outside spaces for playing Frisbee, football, beanbag toss, four square, dodgeball, and any other activities for those who bond best over games and sports. We spend an entire day setting up the residence hall, rearranging furniture, hanging up decorations, and setting out supplies and artifacts to create a space that invites extroverts and introverts, guitar players and painters, athletes and poets, the spiritually curious and the cradle-denominationalists, and adults and youth to find spaces they can both retreat into to feel at home and step into to try new things.

The third choice we make is how to structure our schedule. One of the primary manifestations of our fear of and for youth is our need to pack every waking moment of their schedules with activity, believing that if we keep them busy, they will stay out of trouble. Young people themselves, already well conditioned by a grueling school and extracurricular activity schedule, come to us expecting to be kept busy the entire day. Keeping a Sabbath rhythm each day and each week is both an act of resistance to consumer culture and a faithful response to God's own will for our lives together.[13] So when we design our schedule for the day and for the week, we try to include significant chunks of free time. This free time is often used for napping, exercising, reading, creating artwork, playing cards, putting together puzzles, or just lounging around. Though this time is unprogrammed, it is not unstructured. With the exception of going to one's room to nap or recharge, we encourage community members to use their free time to get to know different people, and our staff is most active during this time, engaging them in conversations, playing games, or just hanging out with them in the lounges, even reading alongside the readers. This is *not* the same as surveillance—staff members are doing these activities alongside the youth, not standing in the back talking to each other and watching the youth.[14] They are building community through sharing stories, discussing ideas, and playing.

The fourth choice we make is to take food seriously. Block makes a point of emphasizing the role of food in creating a hospitable place for gathering, using the language of breaking bread together—the com-*pan*-ionship that Jesus shared during his feeding of the five thousand. He encourages those who want to build transformative community to become conscious of the nutritional and environmental aspects of food because this awareness takes seriously the dignity of the people we have invited to gather. The staple of the youth meeting is pizza, and that is fine—every once in a while. But at YTI, we take seriously the opportunity to learn about new cultures—or about the different cultures our youth come from—by ordering food from a variety of places. We always have fruit and other healthy snacks available, even as we also enjoy cookies and chips. And whenever possible, we cook together or invite members of our community to bake or cook something to share with the group. Of course there are picky eaters, but more often than not, I have witnessed the joy young people derive from proudly explaining their food traditions to the rest of the group, or serving something they have made together, or discovering a new kind of food they never knew about before. The bread we break together is naan, injera, tortillas, and homemade cookies, and the companionship that grows from this goes deeper because of it.

The fifth choice we make is how to issue invitations. Block insists that real transformation can only come through choice.[15] Anyone who has led an event for youth knows the difference between the engagement of young people whose parents pressured them to come and the engagement of young people who show up because youth group is the highlight of their week. We dream of a youth event in which every single participant comes excited, ready to do whatever we have planned, and so enthusiastic they leave to go and convince their friends to join them next time. This dream is in fundamental tension with the demands placed on youth ministry and on youth themselves: parents want us to "fix" their kids, pastors want us to grow the numbers by any means necessary, youth want to participate but are overscheduled and too tired, or they are understandably skeptical about the agendas we may have for them. It takes some courage and self-awareness, but to the extent that we can issue invitations to young people—and adult volunteers—that do not contain underlying pressures to say yes or offer rewards or incentives to come, the more democratic and transformative our youth gatherings will be. Indeed, Block recommends that rather than a reward for coming, invitations should make clear that participation in the gathering has a cost. For those who decide to come, they should know up front that something will be asked of them. This, according to Block, is the best way to build in commitment and accountability from the beginning. At YTI, we have applications to participate. Would-be attendees must complete an application that includes four short essays, one of which asks them to name what sorts of questions and topics they want to explore while at YTI. Once accepted to the program, they sign a commitment form, as do their parents, agreeing to be fully present for the entire program and to come prepared to explore the questions they named in their essays. Of course, we know that many youth come because Atlanta seems like an exciting city to visit, because an older sibling or friend attended, or because their parents or pastors urged them to go. But we ourselves try never to pressure them to come, and we do not promise visits to amusement parks or trips to the mall. We invite them to choose, as freely as possible, to come join us in building a community of theologically and spiritually curious people from around the world.

The sixth choice we make is how to set up small groups. Block sees the small group as "the unit of transformation."[16] No matter how large the gathering is, it is essential to have moments in which participants break into smaller groups (Block suggests about six to twelve per group) so that each person is given space to become known, to get to know others, to share gifts, to offer diverse perspectives, and to raise concerns or questions. At YTI, we have several different kinds of small groups: some that come together based on affinity or interest and some that we construct intentionally to ensure that diverse viewpoints and experiences can be voiced. Our core small group is called "Covenant Group," a group of six to eight youth with two adult conveners who meet regularly in the evenings to reflect on the day's activities, as well as to check in with how each member is doing spiritually, emotionally, and physically. Much prayer and care go into creating these groups: we try to maximize diversity across gender, race, and personality while at the same time making sure that no one in the group is an "only" (e.g., the only female, the only person of color, the only LGBTQIA+ person, the only conservative, the only athlete, etc.). We assign two adults rather than only one as conveners to encourage them to model sharing power and expressing diverse viewpoints. We push them to use small group facilitation tools, such as mutual invitation and circle processes, to ensure that all members of the small group feel welcome to speak, as well as able to listen.[17] These choices, and many others, prepare us for the new thing we want to do with the youth: build together a community where everyone belongs.

Living the Conversations of Belonging: The Journey of Community

Once the youth arrive, we begin the journey of building community together. Block believes that shifts in community come from shifts in conversations and names several kinds of conversations that are essential to creating this shift: conversations around possibility, ownership, dissent and doubt, commitment, and gifts. At YTI, we embody these conversations in a variety of practices and traditions.

The possibility conversation shifts away from problem solving and fixation on the past and toward envisioning an alternative future just beyond reach. It is not dreaming or wishful thinking but an active and public declaration of what can be if we want it. Block believes the possibility conversation "works on us," changing us in the present, making that future a reality. At YTI, we embody this possibility conversation throughout but most explicitly in our opening worship service. Gathering all of the youth who have been trickling in all day, we call them together for a convocation worship service in our sanctuary. While music choices, prayers, and leaders change each summer, two elements are consistent. The first is a welcome statement at the beginning in which we declare that each person in that room, wherever they came from and however much they may in that moment be wondering if they've made the right choice to come, is supposed to be here. We say it slowly, deliberatively, and more than once: each one of you belongs here, you are in the right place, God is working through this gathering, you—*yes you!*—belong here. The second is a short homily in which we declare the possibility of the YTI experience: we are doing a new thing, together. Sometimes I have played with the Galatians language—In Christ "there is neither Jew nor Greek" (Gal 3:28)—inviting them to imagine a community in which in Christ there is neither jock nor geek. I name the diversity in the room: people from different countries; from different parts of the United States; from different denominations and no denominational background; with different gender, ethnic, and racial identities; with different theological and political perspectives. And I proclaim that at YTI, we have the freedom to choose not to divide up into cliques, not to fall into the same patterns of the high school cafeteria, not to be trapped in the roles we have back at home. I proclaim the possibility that we can create a truly inclusive community, if we choose.

The ownership conversation shifts away from passivity and assigning blame to others and toward becoming active citizens who feel a sense of ownership and responsibility for the community. At YTI, ownership is exemplified in our Governance Council. In the narrative at the beginning of this chapter, we saw one moment in a Governance Council meeting, a moment in which two youth representatives, alongside two staff representatives and one staff convener, engaged in making decisions about issues both logistical (changing the schedule) and pastoral (engaging a struggling peer) facing the community. In our early years, we created the Governance Council as an ad hoc council primarily meant to be used in the case of disciplinary issues. What we discovered, however, is that the council members had so much wisdom in how to address community concerns, from minor issues about how to keep the residence hall clean to major issues of conflict among members, that we made it a standing council that met frequently to share insights and make decisions to bring back to the community regularly. Youth are honored, often humbled, to be chosen to serve, and decisions coming from the Governance Council are generally respected because they were made with input from the community, through their representatives. The lesson we aimed to teach through the Governance Council was that this was *their* community and that these decisions were *theirs* to uphold. The lesson we learned was that the young people often had far more creative ideas about how to address an issue than we ever had and that they were capable of weighing the impact of decisions on various members of the community (as well as those outside our community) and the costs and benefits of each decision.

The dissent and doubt conversation shifts away from responding to a community's ideas or plans with lip service, denial, rebellion, or resignation and toward responding to them with integrity and commitment. Block sees the expression of doubt, the raising of concerns and questions, and the welcoming of dissenting views as critical for building a truly transformative community in which everyone feels ownership and belonging. Christians often have a particular reluctance to welcome dissent or doubt, for we are taught that doubt is the opposite of faith and that unity in Christ means the same thing as uniformity in viewpoint. In many churches, we insist that there is only one right answer to deep, complex theological questions—questions that faithful Christians have disagreed over for two thousand years—and we dismiss dissenting views of youth as rebellion, acting out, or being disrespectful. When dissent and doubt are discouraged, people often pay lip service to the plans of a community. They say they are on board but never do anything to make the plan happen. Or they keep silent but find subtle ways to undermine the project. For Block, expressing dissent and articulating doubt are the first steps toward commitment, because if someone can openly raise questions and not be excluded from the community as a result, that person sees that their integrity and dignity matter. They may leave, but if they decide to stay, even as a dissenter, they are committed to the community. And of course, the community will be the wiser for wrestling with serious questions and opposing views. At YTI, our primary pedagogical approach is to prioritize questions over answers. We do not shame or ignore youth when they ask difficult questions about the world, about church, about faith, about religion, or even about God. While they have been trained to expect packaged answers to their questions, we respond differently, taking their questions and doubts seriously, inviting others to wrestle with them, and offering several more questions raised by what they have said. We encourage staff to raise questions as well and take seriously differing views about how we bring more justice into the world, how we live together, how we practice our faith, and how we think about God. We state clearly that questions and doubts will make us stronger, that God is working through our difficult conversations, and that no one has to adopt a particular perspective in order to belong in our community.

The commitment conversation thus shifts away from barter, reward, and punishment and toward making promises to peers—fellow citizens—about how we want to behave with each other and what we are willing to do to make change in the world. Building on these other conversations that encourage ownership and accountability, the commitment conversation is the point in Block's strategy at which members of a community freely choose to commit to something for the good of the whole without expectation of receiving something in return. This is a difficult conversation to embody when we are steeped in a culture that emphasizes self-interest and competition and teaches us that young people are lazy, uncommitted, and must be bribed or cajoled into doing things. At YTI, we try to embody some of this conversation when we invite the youth to develop and abide by community guidelines. As their first activity, our Covenant Groups (discussed above) create a covenant to guide them in the conversations they will have. While most covenants include guidelines such as respecting confidentiality, speaking for oneself without speaking on behalf of entire groups, and listening to each other, it is the process itself, often with significant discussion, that matters. A covenant must be agreed on by all in the group and becomes the basis for accountability as group members become increasingly vulnerable and honest with each other. For the community at large, we begin with basic guidelines written by the staff but invite the youth to discuss and amend them before finalizing them. Once community guidelines are set, we draw on them regularly to remind each other of the promises we have made to each other and the community. Inspired by restorative justice models,[18] we approach occasions of violations of the covenant, as well as other moments of conflict or struggle, by first engaging youth in considering how their actions impact others in the community. We teach the youth and the staff to use nonviolent communication to help them communicate with each other in moments of conflict or breaking of promises.[19] If a problem comes to the Governance Council, we structure the conversation around concern for the safety and well-being of others within the community and emphasize relationships over rules whenever possible. By framing behavioral expectations in terms of commitments to community rather than submission to rules, we have often been able to de-escalate conflicts and keep struggling youth more engaged in the community than they might have been otherwise.

Finally, the gifts conversation shifts the focus from our deficiencies or needs and toward our gifts and what we already have. In particular, Block emphasizes the task of bringing citizens' gifts from the margins to the center and helping citizens acknowledge their own gifts and choose to bring them into the world for the common good. We feel we belong when we realize that our gifts are essential to the community, and we build relationships of trust when we can express to others the ways in which they have blessed us. The delight of working with youth comes from beholding them in moments in which they share their gifts—we love to attend their plays, sports events, and concerts and to see them contribute in worship. But do we notice the gifts that do not usually receive a spotlight? Do we notice and name out loud the gifts they give each other, the gifts they give to us, the gifts they downplay or hide?

One practice we have at YTI is the tradition of palanca bags. Originally derived from a Roman Catholic tradition for confirmation, palanca letters are short notes of encouragement, prayer, and honest communication, intended to "lift up" (*palanca* is Spanish for "lever") the receiver closer to God. At YTI, we have a farewell ritual in which everyone in the community is invited to write palancas to individuals within the community who particularly blessed them during our journey together. These notes are collected in bags, and each participant (staff and youth) receives their bag full of letters as they are leaving to go home. Many years later, alumni and former staff from our program still treasure these letters as small, tangible examples of how they belonged to our community.

WHEN A CROWD BECOMES A COMMUNITY

When Jesus brought the gifts of a young person from the margins to the center, blessing them and sharing them with the crowd, he taught us how to be a transformative community. He wanted us to slow down, break bread together, listen to each other, and make those gifts grow through our own willingness to share with and be accountable to each other. Jesus wanted us to learn how to *belong* to a community—how to feel so welcomed within a group that we wanted to do what we could to see it flourish. This possibility is so radical, so different from what we normally experience, that we often cannot let go of the past enough to let it change our present and future. But if we treat every gathering with young people as a possibility for experiencing yet again what it felt like to break bread on that lush green grass in the presence of Jesus, we might just get a taste of those loaves and fish.

Chapter Three
LEARNING THEOLOGY DELIBERATIVELY

On April 28, 2019, the confirmation class of First United Methodist Church (First UMC), Omaha, made a public statement to the congregation. The eight teenagers, aged thirteen and fourteen, read a letter they had drafted together, in which they began by thanking "all the people who have walked with us during our confirmation year." They noted their "fond memories of singing in the children's choir and watching the kites on Easter morning." They mentioned their "nostalgia about Vacation Bible School and back-to-school picnics with bounce houses on the front lawn." Most important, they wrote, was for them to "have always known that this is where children belong."[1] It is precisely because of their deep formation in this congregation that this particular group of young people felt it necessary to take an unusual step: they refused to be confirmed and officially join their church.

The date is important. The United Methodist Church (UMC) had recently held its Special General Conference, in which a "traditionalist" plan to strengthen the church's ban on LGBTQIA+ ordination and marriage was approved by a narrow margin, a decision that sparked outrage in centrist and progressive UMC circles across the world. In light of their denomination's decision, this group of young people expressed concern that "if we join [the UMC] at this time, we will be sending a message that we approve of this decision." While they emphasized how much they loved their local church, they were clear that they had to "stand up against the unjust actions that the denomination is taking" and that they were "not standing just for ourselves" but standing for "every single member of the

LGBTQ+ community who is hurting right now." They ended their letter by stating, "Because we were raised in this church, we believe that if we all stand together as a whole, we can make a difference."[2]

Several important pieces of this story jump out. First, this is a group of young people *who grew up in the church*. They love their local congregation and have fond memories of the most stereotypical of church-kid activities: bounce houses, vacation Bible school, picnics, and kites. It is clear that their church in many ways is like any number of local congregations across the United States. And yet, precisely *because they were raised in the church*, the youth ended up making a bold and public proclamation on a controversial issue that is dividing their denomination. This particular congregation, First UMC in Omaha, does have a history of acting on this issue: in 1997, then pastor Jimmy Creech performed a same-sex blessing for two women on church grounds and was put on trial and later moved from the church. As a result of this experience, the congregation now has a very active LGBTQIA+ ministry and is engaged in public resistance to its denomination's policies. So this is not an example of young people in *rebellion against* their elders; it is an example of young people applying what they *learned from* their elders to a current issue. And this issue, from the perspective of these young people, is an issue of violence. They felt called to take this action because members of the LGBTQIA+ community are "hurting right now," and they wanted to resist publicly the forces that were causing that harm.[3]

Second, even though this action was a logical outgrowth of the commitments their congregation had already affirmed, it is important to note that the specific action of deciding not to be confirmed and to write a public letter was initiated by the youth themselves. Shortly after the General Conference decision, the youth director informed the pastor that two of the youth wanted to read a statement at the next church council meeting, to be entered into the minutes as a formal expression of dissent. Although outside detractors suggested that the young people did not write the statement themselves, Tim Fickenscher, the confirmation class teacher, told reporters that adults had very little to do with the decision or the wording of the statement: "We tried to give the kids as much latitude in decision-making as we could."[4] After one of the youth brought a draft statement to the church council meeting, read it to the council, and received feedback, the class then continued their conversations as a group and further refined the statement.

Third, this action came at the end of a yearlong process of Christian education. Like many United Methodist youth, the confirmands used the standard *Credo* confirmation curriculum, meeting regularly to explore the history and beliefs of their denomination, tools for theological reflection like the Wesleyan Quadrilateral, and their own Christian vocations.[5] As the youth indicated in their statement, they were "learning about [their] faith and clarifying [their] beliefs."[6] After the General Conference, senior pastor Kent Little met with the entire congregation to explain the decisions that the conference had made and to answer questions. The confirmands attended this meeting, asking questions alongside the adults. Reverend Little then attended the confirmation class itself to talk with the youth in greater detail. At that time, two of the girls in the confirmation class announced that they could not join a denomination that denies LGBTQIA+ people their rights. The confirmation class teacher, Tim Fickenscher, explained to the group what a decision not to join the church would mean—for example, they would not be allowed to vote in church meetings—and that others in the group may have different opinions that had to be considered. Over the course of the next few weeks, the class talked about whether to refuse confirmation as a group or as individuals and worked to refine their public statement. Two weeks before Confirmation Sunday, Reverend Little met with each confirmand individually to review what they had learned in confirmation and to ask each of them directly if they were ready to join the church. Each confirmand told their pastor that, although they loved their local church, they could not join the denomination at this time because of the General Conference decision. He affirmed their decision, and the congregation gave the confirmands a standing ovation when they read their statement in worship. The youth had taken what they were learning in their confirmation class about what it means to be a Christian and a member of the church, weighed the consequences of their decision, worked together to decide on an action, and used their voices to speak up in protest against what they believed to be an act of violence. In other words, they had engaged in a deliberative form of theological exploration that led to public action.

DELIBERATIVE THEOLOGY AS CHRISTIAN DISCIPLESHIP

Our only canonical story about Jesus as a teenager comes from the Gospel of Luke, chapter 2—the story of Jesus in the temple.[7] Though many of us who work with youth might wish we had more stories of Jesus from this age, Luke sets it apart in a way that emphasizes its importance, and its details give us much to consider. Recall that Luke gives the reader many particulars about Jesus's birth and his childhood, more so than any other gospel writer. He then ends his account of Jesus's first phase of life with the phrase "The child grew up and became strong. He was filled with wisdom, and God's favor was on him" (Luke 2:40). Luke closes out the second phase of Jesus's life with similar words by stating, "Jesus matured in wisdom and years, and in favor with God and with people" (2:52). These two verses bracket the story in between them, highlighting Jesus's time in the temple as a critical moment of his growth in wisdom and favor.

The story of Jesus in the temple can easily be told as a story of Jesus's precocity. Of course, we should not be surprised that Jesus—the Son of God—is wise beyond his years and is astounding the people around him; indeed, this is a common trope of hero stories, one that Luke's early readers would have recognized. But this story gives us more than a sneak peek into who Jesus will become when we meet him again after his baptism and temptation in the desert. It shows us a few things about what a teenager who seeks to follow Jesus can do *as a teenager*.

First, when Jesus's parents find him in the temple, they discover him "sitting among the teachers, listening to them and putting questions to them" (Luke 2:46). In other words, Jesus is *learning through deliberative discussion*. There is a give-and-take—he is asking questions and listening to what the others are saying.

Second, he is doing this *with adults*. He is sitting among the most learned in his faith tradition and seeking to grow in wisdom through this process of give-and-take with those who are taking him seriously as an interlocutor.

Third, he is doing this *in public*. The story suggests there are many around who overheard these conversations and were paying close attention, since they were "amazed" by what they saw.

Fourth, this was not just any public space: this was the temple in Jerusalem, the *seat of power* for his religious community.[8]

Jesus the teenager makes a point of engaging in serious theological study, through dialogue, with adults, in public, in the center of power. He is *not* lecturing, or passively receiving a lecture, and he is *not* off in a separate room, away from where the adults are studying. He is where the action is, and the action is doing theology through deliberation and dialogue.

In *How to Think Theologically*, Howard W. Stone and James O. Duke insist that doing theology is at the core of what it means to be a Christian and that doing deliberative theology is the responsibility of all conscientious Christians.[9] For them, every Christian, regardless of age or educational background, is a theologian—"there are no exceptions." When we claim the identity of Christian, we are proclaiming that our lives in some way reflect a set of beliefs. Of course, our actions often do not reflect our aspirations regarding following Jesus, but our actions do reflect something—what Stone and Duke call an "embedded theology." Embedded theology is "the implicit theology that Christians live out in their daily lives." It includes "the theological messages intrinsic in and communicated by praying, preaching, hymn singing, personal conduct, liturgy, social action or inaction, and virtually everything else people say and do in the name of their Christian faith."[10] Because embedded theology is implicit, we are often not aware of how it shapes our actions, but it does. This is the theology we see most often when people argue with each other on social media about abortion or LGBTQIA+ rights or the death penalty or what to do about refugees and immigrants. It is often the theology that informs how and whether we vote, how we engage our families and friends, and the decisions we make in our work and play. We learn it by seeing, hearing, and doing from the moment we join a Christian community—in children's sermons and baptismal liturgies, in retreats and mission trips, in prayers and taking communion, by watching our pastors and the other congregants, and by reading the Bible through the lens of our community.

Most Christians discover at some point that their embedded theology is not enough, however. Sometimes a crisis occurs—someone close to you dies tragically, a natural disaster or political event causes massive suffering, you become close to someone who is not Christian, you become overwhelmed by anxiety or loneliness, you are faced with an ethical dilemma that is not black and white, you read the Bible closely and start to notice uncomfortable contradictions or stories that make your stomach turn—and you realize you have questions your childhood faith cannot answer. Other times, a quiet impulse, what Stone and Duke call "conscientiousness," bubbles up and pushes you to engage Christian beliefs critically in order to deepen and broaden your faith.[11] This marks the point when we turn to deliberative theological reflection.

Deliberative theological reflection is a process of asking critical questions about our embedded theological convictions, and it is a challenge for many Christians to undertake. Deliberative theologians examine what they have taken for granted, consider the widest possible range of alternative understandings, and seek to articulate the meaning of their faith, clearly and coherently, in light of what these new understandings lead them to conclude. It requires humility, for such theologians must be open to the possibility that they can learn from sources they might not have considered before. It requires curiosity, for such theologians must be eager to learn and explore. It requires trust, for such theologians trust that God is with them on this journey, even when doubts threaten to shatter deeply held beliefs and when complexity makes them grieve over lost simplicity. And it requires community, for such theologians cannot discover the full range of alternative understandings without dialogue partners from among the Christian tradition as well as supportive friends and mentors around them.

In our work at the Youth Theological Initiative (YTI), we encourage young people to join us in this practice of deliberative theological reflection. For many years, our tagline was "Exploring Questions That Shape Us." On the application form, we ask youth to name any theological questions they would like to explore while participating in our program. Youth give a variety of answers, but the vast majority are questions with which really smart, deeply faithful Christians have been wrestling since the church began: Why is there suffering and injustice? What happens after we die? What does it mean to lead a good life? What is God's will for my life? Will my Muslim/Jewish/Hindu/atheist friend go to hell?

The joy of doing theology is realizing that once you embark on this deliberative process of asking the harder questions, you don't have to do it alone. As Stone and Duke note, "To engage in theological reflection is to join in an ongoing conversation with others that began long before we ever came along and will continue long after we have passed away."[12] Theology is a "perpetual conversation," and you—yes, you, that young person with questions and doubts and frustrations with the surface-level conversations happening around you—get to be part of it.

Deliberative theological reflection is a process, and Jesus the teenager shows us how to do it. Stone and Duke describe deliberative theological reflection as a process that is "linked by two common techniques: *listening* and *questioning*. Listening involves an active waiting that allows new information in, is prepared to be surprised, and remains open to the illumination of the Spirit. Questioning is a corrective to complacency—the danger of becoming satisfied with old answers and preconceptions.... The aim of listening is receptivity; the aim of questioning is honesty."[13] When Jesus is sitting in the temple, Luke describes him as "listening" and "putting questions" to the scholars around him (Luke 2:46). By both listening and questioning, Jesus the teenager models for us the deliberative posture that Stone and Duke encourage conscientious Christians to adopt. By doing this while sitting among the teachers, Jesus the teenager shows us that deliberative theology is best done not by ourselves but with others who take us seriously as dialogue partners. By doing this in the temple, Jesus the teenager shows us that this work is so important, it must be done at the very center of our institutions, in public, and where the action is.

DELIBERATIVE PEDAGOGY AS AN APPROACH TO THEOLOGICAL REFLECTION AND FAITH FORMATION

While Stone and Duke describe their method of doing theology as deliberative and suggest that the core of deliberation is listening and questioning, the field of deliberative pedagogy refines what the practice of deliberation can mean. *Deliberation* is distinct from both *discussion* and *debate*. According to the Wisconsin Institute for Public Policy and Service, "The goal of discussion is to learn more about a particular topic and strengthen interpersonal relationships" and involves "maintaining a cordial exchange of ideas ... and accepting the views of others without questioning or confrontation."[14] Because a central aim is to get to know each other and build community, discussion will always be an important part of youth fellowship and is often the general process used in Bible study and small groups in churches.

Debate, on the other hand, focuses on "exploration of two different positions, characterized by searching for weaknesses in the other's position, defending your position, [and] valuing the solution to the problem as more important than the relationship between the debaters."[15] The goal of debate is to have a clear winner and loser. In the church, we see this practice used most often when large numbers of members gather to make decisions about policy and church positions on social issues (e.g., AME General Conference, ELCA Churchwide Assembly, TEC General Convention). While it does have value in making it fairly efficient to make a large number of decisions in a concentrated period of time, anyone who has attended a large church gathering where serious disagreement about church policy is present knows that relationships among members suffer greatly in this process.

Deliberation, by contrast, seeks to bring the best of discussion and debate together by "working together to make a decision," using a process that searches for "value in alternative views of the issue." This process enlarges or even changes participants' understanding of the issue, acknowledges "that many people have pieces of the answer and that together participants can develop a workable solution," listens "to understand the priorities and values of others," and weighs the drawbacks and benefits of the various approaches, thus arriving at a goal of finding common ground for action.[16] In other words, deliberation seeks to make significant decisions for action while attending to relationships and learning more about each other and about the topic at hand.

Deliberative pedagogy is a specific set of teaching practices inspired by the goals of deliberation and deliberative democracy.[17] From middle school students discussing what to do about bullying, to high school students wrestling with public policy options for reducing greenhouse gasses in their environmental science class, to college students leading forums with their peers on the challenges of diversity on their campus, young people are already participating in democratic experiments as part of their education. In *Deliberation in the Classroom: Fostering Critical Thinking, Community, and Citizenship in Schools*, Stacie Molnar-Main describes what it looks like to teach deliberation with students:

In classrooms where public deliberation is practiced, learners engage in inquiry about complex issues and participate in deliberative discussions. During deliberative discussions, students consider different perspectives on a social problem, identify and work through tensions related to different approaches to addressing the problem, and attempt to arrive at reasoned judgment together. In contrast to processes that encourage consensus or compromise, the goal of deliberation is not to produce complete agreement among participants. The broad goals, among other curricular goals, are to promote improved understanding of the issue, awareness of the consequences of various responses, and recognition of commonly held values that can inform future action.[18]

Molnar-Main points out that, without the intentional introduction of deliberative practices in the classroom, "it is quite possible that a child could grow up without experiencing an example of democratic politics in which people of different viewpoints work together for the common good."[19] Unlike the toxic spaces on social media, on cable news, in the halls of government, and even in the gatherings of our denominations (and sometimes even families!), the classroom—and perhaps, the youth group room—can become a space for diverse individuals to come together to identify common ground and to connect their learning to civic action.

In addition to the topic under consideration, participants in deliberation learn skills essential for citizens who want to overcome paralysis or complacency and transform the dynamics of violence around them. With practice, participants in deliberation learn to think more flexibly and interdependently, to make personal connections to the issues they discuss, to appreciate others' concerns and experiences, to argue for and evaluate different approaches to problems, to practice agreement and disagreement with others, to find common ground with those who have different views and experiences, and to maintain their own views about an issue, even if they hold views different from others around them. As Molnar-Main notes, young people engaged in deliberative classroom practices "not only practice the skills of listening, speaking, and disagreeing respectfully, but they also learn an approach to problem solving that prepares them to find common ground amid differences."[20] They develop capacities for empathy that we often hope for in discussion and dialogue while at the same time learning how to articulate and make reasoned arguments for the positions they take, what we hope for in encouraging debate. What's more, they can deliberate on courses of action they can take to make positive change, expanding their idea of what it means to be citizens in a democratic system.

Molnar-Main describes six key characteristics for good deliberative learning:

> First, the subject matter should be "an issue of significance to individuals and society" and, ideally, of significance to the students themselves.
> Second, the process of deliberation must be "interactive and discussion based." This is different from presenting students with a range of perspectives in a lecture format.
> Third, participants should "share responsibility for learning," with teachers remaining open to learning from the students during the deliberation process.
> Fourth, the work of deliberating is real work, not role-play. It involves weighing options and making decisions about what actually to do or believe. While members of the group do not need to end up making the same decision, everyone is pushed to decide, and this encourages wrestling with the complexities and messiness of the real world.
> Fifth, "multiple perspectives, including marginalized views, are given balanced consideration." This is the best way to ensure that every student has options from which to choose that best connect to their own views, to prepare

students for encountering different views in other contexts, and to overcome the silence imposed on view takers who differ from the dominant viewpoint.

Finally, students are "treated as citizens or decision makers," often engaging in action as a result of their deliberative discussions. In other words, the decisions that come out of the process do not die in the classroom; they are taken seriously enough to be acted upon in the world.[21]

To aid in keeping the deliberation productive, the National Issues Forums suggests several ground rules. These include (1) that everyone is encouraged to participate, (2) that no one or two individuals dominate the conversation, (3) that the discussion is kept focused on the options under consideration, (4) that the discussion considers all the major choices and positions, (5) that participants maintain an atmosphere for discussion and analysis of alternatives, and (6) that participants remember that listening is as important as talking.[22]

Some teachers have created additional ground rules to help students practice agreeing and disagreeing with each other in productive ways. One teacher, John-Mark Edwards at John Herbert Phillips Academy, asks students to choose one of three ways to respond to what they hear someone else say. They can (1) agree with the person who just spoke and explain why they agree, (2) respectfully disagree and give a reason for disagreeing, or (3) add something to the conversation by building on what has been said. Over time, these practices become habits, and students can then find ways to combine them in more complex ways, such as respectfully disagreeing with one part of what someone says while being able to add something constructive to a piece with which they do agree.[23] By establishing these practices intentionally as part of what it means to consider messy topics in a diverse group, teachers are helping students enter a variety of contexts and contribute positively to decision-making—even when the stakes are high and people disagree strongly.

Deliberative pedagogy thus pays attention to both content and form. Students need materials focused on a particular issue with which to engage, materials that accurately and fairly describe issues that are important to them, that push them to weigh different options, and that expose them to multiple perspectives, including those on the margins. This is the content. Students also need to participate actively in deliberative conversations, feel they can teach as well as learn from others by sharing their perspectives, understand that issues are complex and that good people disagree, see themselves as citizens with power to make change, and feel that the result of the work really matters. This is the form.

The form, or *way* in which we teach, matters as much as, if not more than, the content, or *what* we teach. Deliberative pedagogy teaches students to consider viewpoints different from their own, critically engage their own views to consider what their views might leave out or give up, and move beyond either/or thinking to integrate a variety of perspectives and approaches into new approaches that do not accept an "us versus them" position. This teaches skills in transforming conflict away from division and violence. And because this approach assumes that the students' opinions and decisions matter, that the teachers can change their minds as a result of deliberation alongside the students, that both student and teacher are working together to consider problems and develop solutions, this pedagogy helps young people overcome despair and apathy. Can this technique both enhance the deliberative tradition of theology and teach Christian youth skills in peace building while also helping them mature in their faith?

CREATING NEW MATERIALS FOR SUNDAY SCHOOL: ONE EXAMPLE

Inspired by the reports of classroom teachers using deliberative pedagogy with young people in other fields, I created materials for Sunday school or confirmation classes that use deliberative pedagogy to teach core facets of Christian beliefs and tested them with both youth and adults. For teachers and conveners of deliberative conversations, the creation of quality materials for use with students is critical to success.

In the booklet *Developing Materials for Deliberative Forums,* Brad Rourke outlines a process for preparing "issue guides," handouts, or booklets that participants in a deliberative discussion use as the basis for their deliberations.[24] These issue guides become the primary source of information participants use in considering a wide variety of views and weighing options for decision-making. As such, the materials are most effective when they can provide accessible information that makes the best case for every perspective and that does not push the reader to favor one option over another. They level the playing field by giving everyone who walks into the room the same information to consider. An issue guide is focused on one issue, generally one piece of one issue, to help deliberators focus on actionable decisions.

The two critical elements of an issue guide are "naming" and "framing." The issue guide features a heading that names the issues at stake in ways that do not suggest a single answer. It often starts with a broad theme and then develops an open-ended question based on that theme, which, if answered, would require citizen action. Essentially, when we name an issue, we ask, "What should we do?" The issue guide then provides a framework for thinking about answering this big question. The framework lists the options or perspectives used to understand an issue or problem, as well as critical information, drawbacks, and trade-offs associated with different approaches. Ideally, the guide should feature three or four broad perspectives to be explored. Providing only two perspectives leads to debate and polarization, so having three or four allows people to break out of the typical divisions we find in many of our political conversations today. The perspectives should use the everyday language that people employ to talk about the issue. Ideally, the approaches should not align with partisan framings or the views of specific individuals or groups and should include major as well as marginalized perspectives.

The guides should include links to primary and secondary sources that represent different perspectives on the themes and allow participants to check sources and learn more on their own. Most important, the descriptions of the three or four approaches should include key information about each approach, sample actions of what those approaches involve, and some information about the strengths and limitations of each option, as well as the trade-offs that would have to be made if that approach were adopted. Essentially, when we frame an issue, we ask, "If we adopt this approach or action, what consequences should we take into account, and given our understanding of both the advantages and trade-offs, are we willing to live with the trade-offs because the advantages outweigh them?"

In the example described below, I chose the issue "Who is Jesus?" This issue goes to the core of what Christians must wrestle with if they want to move from embedded theology to deliberative theology and relates to my discussion of the role of christological images in the introduction. It matters that Starr Carter in *The Hate U Give* prays to Black Jesus, and it matters for our youth to consider what images of Jesus shape their faith. I chose this issue as well because it resonated with youth and youth workers. Rourke notes, "If the materials are to support public deliberation, they must begin where the public does."[25] Questions about who Jesus is preoccupy many people in "the public"—that is, in the church.

Rourke also notes that effective materials must "take into account citizens' various starting points and chief concerns," and writers of these materials cannot skip the step of actually going out and talking to citizens to find out what really concerns them about a given topic.[26] In order to emulate this process and ask a more pointed question about Jesus's identity, I created an online group of youth workers, young adults, and youth from a range of perspectives across denominations, life experiences, socioeconomic and racial backgrounds, and gender identities—playfully called "the Conclave." I asked members of the Conclave questions based on Rourke's template:

> When you think about what you have been taught about who Jesus is, what concerns you? What bothers you most, personally?
> What concerns do you hear friends, family members, or others talking about when it comes to what they've been taught about who Jesus is?

Conclave members gave me a range of responses. Some were concerned that the image of Jesus taught to them was one of an exclusive personal savior, which made it difficult for them to connect Jesus to public action and hard to know what to do about friends and family who were not Christian. Others were concerned that they saw too many people around them using Jesus's teachings in ways that marginalized others. Several noted that the image of Jesus as a white male made it difficult for them to develop a relationship with him, either because they were themselves men and had barriers to developing intimate relationships with other men or because they found it difficult to relate to a savior who looked like their oppressor. Still others expressed concerns that Jesus was simply not talked about enough by their friends and family, limiting the impact of Jesus's salvific power to fewer and fewer people.

Noting some of the underlying concerns Conclave members expressed—fears that images of Jesus created barriers to people developing a personal relationship with him, portrayed him as so personal and private that people could not make connections between their relationship with Jesus and their calling to act in the world as followers of Jesus, had been misused to exclude or harm people, and made him too perfect or too abstract for anyone to follow—I used Rourke's template to create an issue guide.

Rourke notes that an issue guide usually contains five elements: The first is a *title* that reflects the major tension inherent in the issue and conveys that there is a difficult question or problem that must be faced. I titled my issue guide "Our Images of Jesus," with a subheading that asks the question, "How do we think of Jesus in ways that transform our lives *and* the world?" My intent was to note the tension I observed between images of Jesus that youth found personally transformative and images that encouraged them to practice a social ethic inspired by Jesus's earthly ministry.

The second element is an *introduction* that explains what the issue is and why something must be done about it. I began by noting the multiplicity of images of Jesus in the Bible and Christian tradition and that these images have been both a help and a hindrance for faith. I then framed the problem as follows:

> When we pray to or think about Jesus, we have an image in our minds of who he is, what he looks like, and how he relates to us and to other people. The problem that must be faced is that we all have images of Jesus we have developed through our life experiences and what we've learned, and these images impact not only our faith but our actions in the world. The images most dear to us might actually do harm to other people. The images most dear to others might do harm to us. While we might want to say that Jesus is a universal figure, because Jesus was fully human and came to earth in a specific time and place, images of Jesus are particular and cannot remain vague. Jesus was a *particular human being* in a *particular body*, and that has implications, especially if we claim that this particular human was also God. This particularity of Jesus on earth is part of why we have such a rich tradition of artistic depictions of Jesus, through paintings, statues, music lyrics, and illustrations in our vacation Bible school and Sunday school materials. But these images shape our imaginations of who Jesus is, and this has consequences.

I then suggested that a decision of import must be made: "As maturing Christians, we must deliberatively choose an image of Jesus Christ as the focus of our faith and model for our spiritual growth.

How we image Jesus matters: it influences how we understand what it means to follow Jesus, it influences how we treat others who believe differently from us, it influences whether we really believe Jesus loves us and others. . . . As maturing Christians, it is our challenge to enter into this conversation and make our own thoughtful, prayerful decisions about what to do."

The main body of the issue advisory then features four choices to consider related to how to image Jesus. It includes Rourke's recommended third element, descriptions of each *option* for dealing with the issue, and the fourth and fifth elements, two *subsections* under these options that feature examples of *actions* or *benefits* that follow from choosing that option and examples of *drawbacks* or *trade-offs* inherent in each action. In my adaptation, I changed the subsection language of "benefits" and "drawbacks" to "life-giving" and "challenging" and tied it to the action of maturing as a Christian (i.e., spiritual growth). The four options for deliberation I included were to focus on Jesus (1) as our friend, (2) as a martyr who died for us, (3) as a teacher and healer, or (4) as God's Son, the Second person of the Trinity. For each option, I began with a scriptural passage that illustrated the option, placing them all as equally valid, and equally biblical, options.[27] I then included a short paragraph that connects the biblical passage with the overall image of Jesus proposed and then listed several reasons each image can be "life-giving for maturing Christians" and several reasons this image can also be "challenging for maturing Christians." These points of benefits/drawbacks are informed by theological scholarship, as well as by insights gleaned from the Conclave and from conversations with youth at YTI. I ended each option description with a set of questions for the group to consider, designed to encourage appreciation of the image and of those fellow Christians who prefer this image, raise critical questions about the image, and push participants to weigh the trade-offs that come with this option, all while encouraging perspective taking and awareness of the diversity of Christian beliefs and practices:

What is appealing about this image of Jesus? What do you
  imagine is appealing about this image for other Christians?
What concerns you about this image of Jesus? What concerns
  do you imagine other Christians might have about this
  image?
If you made this the primary image of Jesus to focus on for
  your spiritual growth, what would you be giving up? What
  concerns would you be ignoring?

In the final section of the issue advisory, I listed several questions for group reflection designed to encourage consideration of shared values within the group, deliberation about what is gained and lost with each choice, and moving toward a group decision:

Can we identify any shared values among some or all of these
  different images of Jesus Christ?
Can we identify any shared values among our own group?
  What do we value most in how we think about Jesus Christ?
Can we identify any trade-offs or downsides that some or all of
  us are willing (or not willing) to make when we think about
  our images of Jesus Christ?
Is there one image of Jesus Christ we would like to lift up as
  most important to our faith journey at this moment in the life
  of our group? Why?

Although a decision to choose only one image of Jesus on which to focus is not mandatory, the push to make at least a provisional decision to focus in a particular direction through a group process of weighing the consequences of each choice is what makes this exercise truly deliberative. Within a youth group setting, making a choice might then inform what images of Jesus to use when decorating the youth room, where to focus their next Bible study, how to approach prayer—or how youth will show what image of Jesus they are following by how they treat others or interpret current events.

REIMAGINING CONFIRMATION AND SUNDAY SCHOOL?

In her essay "Deep Democracy: The Inner Practice of Civic Engagement," Patricia A. Wilson notes, "At its essence, deep democracy is the inner experience of interconnectedness." Democracy is "deep" when the individual experiences the "enfranchisement of self at the level of mind, heart, and spirit: the realization that 'I count.'" One realizes that one "counts" upon discovering that one is a member of a larger whole and accepts "responsibility for that whole, and the desire to act for the good of the whole: the realization that 'I care.'" This is, in essence, what Peter Block suggests in the dual meaning of "belonging": to be at home (to count) and to take ownership (to care). Wilson describes deep democracy as individuals and community coming together in a creative tension "held in place by the transformation of self through greater understanding of, compassion for, and relationship with an expanding circle of others."[28] In his first letter to the Corinthians, the apostle Paul describes communion with Jesus Christ and his followers as a body with many diverse parts, inextricably interconnected and necessary to the functioning of the body—Christians, as members of the body of Christ, both "count" as individual members and "care" about every other member, knowing that "God has put the body together, giving greater honor to the part with less honor so that there won't be division in the body and so the parts might have mutual concern for each other. If one part suffers, all the parts suffer with it; if one part gets the glory, all the parts celebrate with it" (1 Cor 12:24–26). Can some of the insights from teaching deliberative democracy help us learn what it means to be parts of Christ's body?

As a method of teaching, deliberative pedagogy can be used to teach a wide range of content and has been used to teach social science, science, and humanities courses. Presumably, then, it can also be used to teach theology. In my example above, I have attempted to create one way of using deliberative pedagogy to encourage young people to think critically and compassionately about what is at stake in how we image Jesus, but such materials can also be created to consider different understandings of the atonement, life after death, Jesus's racial and gender identity, our relationship to God's creation, how to relate to other religions, and many other "big questions" that young people already wonder about but rarely find the space and permission to explore deliberatively.

What if confirmation classes, Bible study, or Sunday school meetings were like this? Could you create deliberative theological issue guides on specific aspects of your church's doctrines that you want your youth (or adults) to consider? What if you trained some of your youth leaders to lead these discussions with their peers? This might be a way of growing in maturity and wisdom the way Jesus did—deliberatively, with adults taking them seriously, in public, and in the center of their religious community.

Might you end up with a group of young people refusing to be confirmed, as with First UMC Omaha? Possibly. But when was the last time a group of middle school students thought what they believed was so important that they had to take a stand publicly to live that out?

Chapter Four
READING THE BIBLE CACOPHONOUSLY

"OK, did everybody understand that? Any questions?"

Lauren Calvin Cooke had just asked her small seventh grade girls' group to read aloud the third chapter of the Gospel of John. This was the third week of their Bible study of the Fourth Gospel. Though on the whole, Lauren thought the meetings were going well, she was well aware that John's Gospel, with its metaphysical orientation and metaphorical language, was difficult to understand. Chapter 3, the story of Jesus's conversation with Nicodemus and the location of "Everyone's Favorite Bible Verse" (John 3:16), was such a deeply influential source of theology for her church that Lauren wanted to do more than simply "cover" the text and move on. She wanted the students to dig into it, look at it from multiple perspectives, connect it to their lives—and yes, ask questions.

"OK, did everybody understand that? Any questions?"

Nodding their heads, the students assured her that they understood. They didn't have any questions. Lauren was not convinced. She tried again.

"Really?"

A few started to admit that maybe there were some things they didn't fully understand. Leading by example, Lauren admitted, "'Cause I don't really understand much of it at all."

By modeling her own willingness to admit that the text was hard to understand, the students started opening up.

"Yeah, I didn't understand any of it either."

With this door now open, Lauren tried something new with her group. Rather than asking *if* they had questions—an opening she now realized closed down conversation too early—she invited them to share the questions she knew they had but were afraid to ask. She passed out blank index cards and pens and asked them each to write down at least one question they had about the passage. The wait was painful. After a full five minutes of awkward silence, one girl finally came up with one question: "What does this entire passage mean?" Lauren asked them to try again. To be more specific. To ask questions about particular details that didn't make sense to them, information that seemed to be missing, vocabulary words they didn't know, things they were wondering about as a result of something they saw in the passage.

After a while, the questions started to flow: "Why did Nicodemus come at night? Does Nicodemus ever come up in the Bible again? Who are the Pharisees? What does it mean that Jesus is God's *Son*?" And the more they probed, the deeper it got: "If Jesus is God, when Jesus died, does that mean that there was no God for three days? Where did God come from, anyway? Why do we believe Jesus was God? Why don't Muslims believe that? How different is Christianity from Islam, anyway, since we all trace back to Abraham?"

Thrilled by this new level of engagement, Lauren decided to use index cards every week to jump-start the conversation. Though not all students shared with the group the questions they had written on their cards, those who did began to take risks, asking questions they had not dared to raise previously. Often preceded by disclaimers such as "This may be an irreverent question to ask, but . . ." and "I don't know if I'm allowed to ask this, but . . . ," these questions cut to the very heart of what the youth were really wondering—about the world, about God, about their lives.

Lauren expanded this practice with other Bible study groups of different ages and through it, stumbled into some profound insights. For example, when the middle school girls got to John 8, the story of Jesus and the woman caught in adultery, one twelve-year-old girl asked, "Where was the man she was having an affair with? Why didn't they want to kill him too?" This question not only dug deep enough to notice what was missing from the text; it also opened up a conversation about contemporary experiences of sexism. Even more, it led the girls back to a new insight about Jesus. One student concluded from the story that "unlike a lot of people in our culture, Jesus doesn't blame women more than men—he treats them equally."

Sometimes the question method made it possible for students to disagree over their interpretations of the text, driving them back to the text to read more closely. When looking at the death of Lazarus in John 11, one student asked the question, "Why did Jesus let Lazarus die?" to which another student answered, "So that his sisters would believe." However, another student noticed that the text indicated that Mary and Martha already believed before Lazarus's death, which pushed all of the students to reconsider the first interpretation and review the text to seek out different ones.

At other times, students felt freed by the conversation to offer their own insights, based on their personal experiences. In a study of Exodus, one student asked a question about why God would have chosen Moses to lead the Israelites out of Egypt. Another student, who identified as a "third-culture kid" (a young person who has grown up in a culture other than their country of nationality for a significant part of their early years and who often does not feel totally at home in either culture), stated that it was obvious why Moses was chosen: as a third-culture kid raised by Egyptians but descended from Hebrews, he was the perfect bridge-person to negotiate between Pharaoh and the Israelites. The middle school girls, reading about John's images of Jesus as the Vine, began to brainstorm other metaphors for Jesus and landed on images of Jesus as mother, drawing on their own experiences of being children and being young women who might someday become mothers. When reading about the man born blind, one student asked, "If God loves us all, why are some people born with a disability?" Another student, whose brother has a disability, answered, "Maybe being born with a disability is not a bad thing. Maybe God loves diversity."

And then students started to ask the really risky questions. One day, a student asked the eternal burning question of all monotheists: "If God is good and all-powerful, why do bad things happen to good people?" One student blurted out, "What if God is actually bad, but we let God off the hook?" While the other students, scandalized by the irreverent question and with eyes wide and mouths agape, looked to Lauren to see how she would respond, Lauren simply pointed them to another text—Job—to show them that yes, even this question was safe to ask in this space and in fact was included within the Bible itself.

Once the students realized that even this question could be on the table, the questions spilled out, venturing into areas other than Scripture. They began asking questions about the pastor's sermons. Then church policies. Then about current cultural and political issues. A few questions on an index card, along with a willingness to make space for them, had transformed Bible study into a space for young people to learn how to speak up. Bible study became a site for teaching the skills to overcome silence that results from images of youth as incomplete adults who cannot handle difficult ideas and transform the violence that results from theologies that fear precocious delinquents who point out paradox, ask tough questions, and wrestle with a dynamic, living God.

A GREEK-SPEAKING JEW AND AN ETHIOPIAN EUNUCH READ SCRIPTURE TOGETHER

"Bible study" as we know it today did not exist in first-century Palestine, but the faithful Jews of the time—the ones with whom Jesus argued, many of the disciples themselves, and Jesus himself—knew their sacred texts backward and forward. Jesus's words are steeped in the Torah, Psalms, and Prophets, and he uses and adapts these texts to fight off Satan in the wilderness (Matt 4:1–11), argue with his opponents (John 6:45; Mark 10:1–9), teach his many disciples (Matt 5:3–48), and cry out to God from the cross (Mark 15:34; Luke 23:46). In Luke 4:14–21, we even see Jesus pick up a written scroll, as he reads from Isaiah to proclaim the good news to be fulfilled as they hear his reading. We do not, however, see two people studying a written text together, wrestling with it to understand how it connects with their faith, until we get to the carriage of the Ethiopian eunuch in Acts 8:26–40.

The story of Philip's encounter with the Ethiopian eunuch often serves as the paradigmatic story of evangelism. In it, an angel from the Lord tells Philip to go down the road headed southwest from Jerusalem toward Gaza, where, led by the Spirit, he approaches an Ethiopian man sitting in a carriage, reading aloud from the prophet Isaiah. Philip asks the man if he understands what he is reading, and when the man says no and invites him into his carriage, Philip hops in and begins to help him understand Isaiah in light of the good news of Jesus Christ. The man sees water and asks if he can be baptized on the spot. Philip does this, the Spirit immediately whisks him away to Azotus, and he continues his evangelizing up the coast toward Caesarea. The Ethiopian "went on his way rejoicing" (Acts 8:39), back to his Ethiopian queen and court, perhaps to spread the good news there as well.

Yet besides being a model for evangelism, this story is also a story about reading Scripture together, and a closer look at some of the details reveals important insights we can use to consider Bible study today. First, the physical format of the Scriptures we read matters. The Ethiopian official is reading aloud from a scroll—not a bound book containing all the Jewish Scriptures in one place and certainly not any writings that Christians call the New Testament. Most likely, all he had was an Isaiah scroll, tightly wound in a way that precluded him from jumping around to different parts of Isaiah and making it impossible to look up passages from other writings. Actual sacred texts like this would be rare and expensive and normally found only in synagogues as communal property; he must have been very privileged to have his own copy and even more privileged to be literate enough to read it. These material considerations affect his encounter with the text—a point to which we return shortly.

Second, the culture and identity of those involved in Bible study shape their encounter with the text. The Ethiopian, whose name we never learn, is described quite specifically as "an Ethiopian man," a "eunuch," and "an official responsible for the entire treasury of Candace," the Ethiopian queen, and who was on his way home after having worshipped in Jerusalem (Acts 8:27). Though scholars do not agree on the full significance of all these aspects of his identity, it is noteworthy that the author of Acts wants us to know about this man's ethnicity, political allegiance, gender identity, class status, and religious practices. As an Ethiopian, he represents a powerful, even dangerous, far-off land and has black skin, which Roman readers of the time considered exotic and possibly suspect. He is the chief financial officer for the queen, is riding in a carriage with servants, and possesses a written scroll, suggesting significant political power and class privilege. At the same time, as a eunuch, we know that he should have been excluded from full participation in temple worship and represents an ambiguous gender and sexual identity, one outside the procreative, patriarchal system. We don't know if he is a Jew, a proselyte, or a gentile "God-fearer," but he is clearly serious about his religious practice, having traveled so far to get to Jerusalem and reading so intently in Isaiah. The passage that the Ethiopian was reading, Isaiah 53:7–8, comes from the Suffering Servant songs, in which the prophet describes someone who was like a sheep led to the slaughter, who was humiliated, and for whom justice was taken away. It is possible that the Ethiopian wondered if the prophet could be referring to someone like himself, someone who also has been "humiliated" in his manhood as a eunuch. If he had been reading further ahead in the scroll, in Isaiah 56:3–8, in which the Lord says that "eunuchs who keep my sabbaths" and the "immigrants who have joined me" will be gathered in as God's people, he may have wondered if this gathering would also include him.

Though perhaps less obvious, Philip likewise comes to the text shaped by his own identity. We learn from Acts 6 that Philip has been chosen as one of seven men "endowed by the Spirit with exceptional wisdom" (Acts 6:3) to attend to the Greek-speaking or hellenized portion of the new Jesus-following community, presumably because he was himself a hellenized Jew. This makes him a bridge-figure between gentiles and Jews, and this contributes to his success in evangelizing in Samaria at the start of Acts 8. As someone designated to serve, guided by the Spirit, and as someone who himself may have been on the margins of the Aramaic speaking community, Philip surely climbs into the carriage hoping that he can be that bridge-person who can seize the "teachable moment" and fulfill his calling to share a new reading of Scripture with a person so different from him. Both men are looking to Isaiah for good news on who is included in God's people. Both have something at stake in the answer.

Third, the best way to study Scripture is to ask questions while reading with others. As Philip runs up to the carriage, he can hear the Ethiopian man reading Isaiah aloud and, as Lauren did of her girls' Bible study group, asks him, "Do you really understand what you are reading?" (Acts 8:30). The man, both wise and humble, admits that he does not and responds with his own question: "Without someone to guide me, how could I?" (8:31). As he invites Philip to climb up and sit with him, he shows Philip the passage and asks yet another question: "Tell me, about whom does the prophet say this? Is he talking about himself or someone else?" (8:34). Philip's question opens up the space to explore. The Ethiopian's questions signal an openness to explore together, and then dive right into the messiness of that joint exploration. Questions, it seems, bring people together to study Scripture more deeply.

Fourth, studying Scripture is risky but worth it. Philip takes significant risks to obey God and approach the Ethiopian. Just before he receives a command from an angel of the Lord, Philip has been working in Samaria. He and other disciples are scattered throughout the region after Stephen has been killed and persecution has increased. The angel tells him to go to a desolate, lonely road on the way to Gaza and gives him no further information until he gets there. The Spirit tells him to approach a carriage, again with no further information. Despite the fact that he is part of a persecuted movement and is walking alone in a dangerous area, Philip takes the risk to approach the carriage. Likewise, the Ethiopian, who has just been interrupted in his reading by a random, unknown man who approached him on the road, and who is himself traveling in a foreign land, invites this stranger into his private cabin, exposing himself to danger. Both men make themselves vulnerable to each other in order to make way for the Holy Spirit to work within them through the text. The Spirit shows up in the encounter, and they part rejoicing (Acts 8:39)!

What if Philip had played it safe and stayed away from the road? What if the Ethiopian had asked the driver to keep going to avoid this pestering stranger?

Fifth, wrestling with Scripture leads to action. Through this encounter, the Ethiopian eunuch is immediately converted and wants to seal this with baptism. As they approach the water, he asks yet one more question: "What would keep me from being baptized?" (Acts 8:36). Presumably, he worries that something would—most likely because he is a eunuch, or perhaps because he is a foreigner or a person of color. But Philip raises no objection, and they both act immediately in response to the good news they find in the text. What's more, the action continues for both of them, as Philip is whisked away by the Spirit to continue his evangelizing work, and the Ethiopian goes home, empowered to share with others the good news he has found.

OVERCOMING SILENCE BY READING THE BIBLE CACOPHONOUSLY

Scholar and religion professor Timothy Beal points out that "the Bible," as many of us think of it, is a bankrupt idea, and it actually prevents us from growing in our faith. Tracing the history of the development of the book we now call "the Bible," Beal reminds us that—just as we saw with the Ethiopian eunuch—the physical forms of sacred writings were radically different for the ancient Israelites and the early Christians than they are for us today. Before the fourth century CE, "the Bible" as a single book was not possible. Technologically, it was not possible because paper as we know it did not exist in this part of the world (though it did in China). Binding together multiple pages made of animal skins or papyrus was heavy and expensive and could not hold in one place the hundreds of pages of biblical writings we know today in a way that anyone could carry. Literarily, it was not possible because an agreed-upon canon did not exist. A wide variety of writings, and versions of writings, competed with each other for adherents, and it was not until an imperial Christianity possessed the power, and the new technology of bookbinding, to force a unity from such diversity that a canon took form.[1] The idea of "the Bible" as a single immutable text that speaks with one voice, in terms that can be understood easily and literally, about everything we need to know, and exclusive of other sources of knowledge, is a recent historical phenomenon, arising in the nineteenth century as a response to industrialization, immigration, and the scientific study of sacred texts, and this Bible bears no resemblance to the way Jesus, King David, Philip, or the Ethiopian read sacred texts.[2]

This more recent view of "the Bible" is what Beal calls a "cultural icon." By making the Bible a cultural icon, we have actually created an idol—a god that promises absolute certainty and simplistic morality in exchange for obedient adherence to one interpretation. This has been dangerous for the faith development of Christians. Beal states, "The iconic idea of the Bible as a book of black-and-white answers encourages us to remain in a state of spiritual immaturity. It discourages curiosity in the terra incognita of biblical literature, handing us a Magic 8 Ball Bible to play with instead. In turning readers away from the struggle, from wrestling with the rich complexity of biblical literature and its history, in which there are no easy answers, it perpetuates an adolescent faith."[3]

Beal uses his own experience growing up as a teenager to point to the problems this view of the Bible has created for young people. Having been told that all the answers he needed about life would be found easily and clearly in the Bible, he discovered that when he actually tried to read it, he quickly became discouraged. The heroes he heard about in Sunday school—Abraham, Moses, David—were far from perfect and often achieved greatness through murder and trickery. Different parts of the Bible said conflicting things. Many passages simply did not make sense to him. He knew the Bible was supposed to be "God's textbook for the world," but he couldn't find in it clear, simple answers to his questions.[4]

So he stopped reading. And so, he notices, have many of the students he teaches now. Because they believed that the Bible is supposed to give clear answers to all questions—and only one answer for each question—these young people blame themselves when they can't find those answers. Beal describes a cycle of trying to read, experiencing difficulty, assuming you are too sinful or too stupid to get it, being told that your questions are not welcome in church, and giving up. In other words, because we have made the Bible into a cultural icon—an idol—we have discouraged people from asking questions, wrestling with contradiction and paradox, sitting with diverse viewpoints, and diving into a process of deep engagement with the richness of the text that would, in fact, lead to spiritual maturity.

As an antidote to this, Beal proposes that we see the Bible not as a Magic 8 Ball that we use to give us simple answers to life's questions but instead as a "library of questions." The Bible thus becomes a place into which we enter to find a vast array of different voices that we can never completely master, but a place in which we can spend a lifetime discovering new places to start reading and new insights along the way. Such a place, "in its failure to give clear answers and its refusal to be contained by any synopsis or conclusion, points beyond itself to mystery, which is at the heart of the life of faith." Such a place, moreover, creates community because it invites everyone to enter at different points, to pull down different books from the shelves, to wrestle with these texts and with each other in a "creative, meaning-making process of interpretation" that is messy but held together by our common journey and by our interdependence in helping each other grow in wisdom as we learn together. This kind of reading draws on much deeper roots than the modern cultural icon of the Bible; it draws on traditional rabbinic practices of studying sacred texts through dialogue, questioning, and even debate—with each other and with the text. Beal paints a picture of the Jewish beit midrash—the study halls in Jewish education in which dozens of students study Scripture in pairs, all in one room, passionately discussing their interpretations with each other. Such an "endless, inarticulate din of talking, arguing, reading, and re-reading in the library of questions" becomes a "cacophonous hymn" to God.[5] By reading the Bible cacophonously, we can begin to overcome the silence young people often face when they are discouraged from asking questions about the text.

TRANSFORMING VIOLENCE BY READING THE BIBLE INTERCULTURALLY

While the cultural icon of the Bible as a unified voice with easy-to-find answers has silenced the diversity of questions we bring to our study of Scripture, the dominance of biblical interpretation by Europeans, enforced on other peoples through the close cooperation of colonialism and mission, and through Western dominance of the practices of scholarly biblical interpretation, has silenced the "great polyphony of different cultural voices" within, around, and in response to biblical texts,[6] committing a kind of "interpretive violence" against women and sexual minorities, people with disabilities, people of color, and peoples from different cultural contexts. Choi Hee An notes that the Bible has always been the object of multiple and diverse readings but that these readings are erased when we assume the Bible speaks with one voice and can be interpreted only through the lens of Western culture and Western Christian tradition.[7] When only one kind of reading prevails, those who have the most power and privilege—whites, males, wealthy people, imperial centers, and so on—come to see themselves as the center of the story, as the "we" to whom the Bible is speaking. Those with less power—people of color; women; those in poverty, with disabilities, from colonized countries; and so on—come to be seen as the "them" or the "others" that the "we" define themselves against. It then becomes very easy for people to use the Bible to perpetuate racism, classism, sexism, heterosexism, ableism, ageism, and colonialism. As Johanna W. H. van Wijk-Bos notes, *how* we read the text, not just *what* we read, shapes our actions.[8] To be peace builders who can transform violence, we must attend to *how* we read the Bible and how history, culture, and identity shaped not only the way in which the writers and redactors of the Bible formulated these texts but also the ways in which communities continue to interpret and use them.

As a solution to this "interpretive violence," Fernando Segovia proposes that we adopt a "hermeneutics of otherness and engagement," in which we take seriously the distinctiveness of the varieties of biblical voices and interpretations of these voices without forcing them into a single interpretation for all times, all places, and all people. In response to two centuries of biblical scholarship dominated by a European exegetical method that has assumed a neutral, universal reader (yet a reader who by default comes to resemble Western white men), Segovia insists that we acknowledge the "flesh-and-blood reader" who is "always situated and engaged, socially and historically conditioned, reading and interpreting from a variety of different and complex social locations." At the same time, each reader should acknowledge that the text itself is a product of writers, redactors, editors, transcribers, and translators who themselves are always socially, historically, and culturally conditioned as well. Because every text and every reader are all shaped by their "social locations," we must move away from practices in which only one reader and one interpretation are allowed to be authoritative. We do this by committing "to see readers, all readers and readings, as distinct and autonomous voices"—recognizing their otherness—and by committing to "critical dialogue and exchange with the other, subjecting our respective views of one another and the world to critical exposure and analysis," embarking on engagement.[9] This hermeneutics of otherness and engagement thus pushes us to consider critically not only the diverse perspectives *within* the Bible but also the diverse perspectives within the history of biblical interpretation and the diverse perspectives within our own Bible study group. By reading the Bible interculturally, we can begin to transform the violence wrought by harmful biblical interpretations and by the insistence that only one reading is faithful and true.

CACOPHONOUS QUESTIONS

When we treat the Bible as if it were "God's textbook," a source that speaks directly and unambiguously about everything from dating to career choices to current social debates, we set young people up for disillusionment when they actually try to read it and discover how messy and cacophonous it actually is. When we imply that the Bible is a book of simple answers, we also imply that questions are somehow a sign of weak faith, discouraging youth from asking the big questions about life, God, and the world that leads to true wisdom and spiritual growth. When we imply that the Bible speaks with one voice, we silence the many diverse voices within Scripture itself. When we approach the Bible as a cultural icon rather than a library of questions, we silence youth, we silence people who disagree with us, and we silence the many voices of the saints who have journeyed with God for thousands of years, wrestling with the hard, messy realities of living a life of faith in a complex world. To overcome silence, we must welcome noise. We do that by making questions the heart of Bible study.

In this chapter's opening vignette, we met Lauren Calvin Cooke. Based on her experience developing her "question method" with her youth group, she offers several important suggestions for facilitating the method described above.[10] Calvin Cooke recommends asking, "What questions do you have?" (as opposed to "Do you have any questions?") in order to avoid "yes/no" answers and to establish question asking as the normal posture toward reading the Bible. The leader should then allow time for students to write on their index cards or think about their questions. Calvin Cooke recommends at least twenty seconds of silence—a span of dead air that might feel excruciatingly long but is necessary to give introverts and students unused to asking questions about the Bible time to formulate their thoughts. If questions are of a factual nature that can be answered by referring to a Bible dictionary, a concordance, a map, or an online search, the facilitator can encourage the students to look up the answers—a little tutorial on how to use these tools, whose repeated practice will teach them skills to use for the rest of their faith journey. If they are easy to answer off the top of her head, the facilitator may do so—sparingly. She should try not to play the role of "Bible expert" too often, as it is better to show youth how to find their own answers than to continue to send the message that they should rely on one person for information.

Questions that wonder about theological ideas or ethical dilemmas, try to make connections to the current context, explore historical or literary dimensions of the text, or note what is not in the text are all questions that the facilitator should not answer right away, or possibly at all. Calvin Cooke urges us to "treat student questions like boomerangs, immediately throwing [them] back to the group for further reflection," by saying, "Ooh, hmm. That's a good question. What do you all think?" which indicates that the question is sufficiently important to pause over, affirms students in asking questions, and invites the rest of the group to wrestle with the question together. By refraining to be the first to share—putting questions back to the group rather than answering them herself and, when enough students have shared, only then offering her opinion "as a helpful contribution, not a definitive answer"—the facilitator can slowly shift students away from seeing the Bible as a Magic 8 Ball, with the Bible teacher as a guru with all the answers, and toward seeing the Bible as a library of questions, with the Bible teacher as a librarian who can open the doors and show them the rich array of questions waiting for them on the shelves.

INTERCULTURAL INVENTORIES

When we treat the Bible as a univocal and unambiguous "textbook" rather than a rich library of questions, we also send the message that readers should only arrive at one univocal and unambiguous reading of each text. When we assume that a passage or story in the Bible can only be interpreted in one way, that "one way" defaults to the way established by those in power. Historically, that has been white Western men. Reading the Bible has consequences, not just for our souls, but also for our bodies and for the bodies and souls of those who have been on the receiving end of policies that have portrayed one group of people as "God-ordained" to subjugate other groups of people. When we imply that there is only one way to interpret a passage, we send a message—however inadvertently—that those who read the passage differently, or who become the "Other" in a particular interpretation, are not just wrong but on the wrong side, on a different side than God. It does not take long before this kind of thinking justifies dehumanizing other people and committing violence against them—consider attacks on Jews as "Christ killers"; the support of chattel slavery as the "curse of Ham"; the taking of lands from Indigenous "Canaanite" peoples in North America, Southern Africa, and Palestine; the silencing of women in the church; and the spiritual abuse of LGBTQIA+ Christians as but a few examples.[11]

At the Youth Theological Initiative (YTI), a program that gathers youth from a wide range of theological and cultural backgrounds, we seek to help students see the importance of identity and culture in reading the Bible. Based on a practice used at New York Theological Seminary, the authors of *The Peoples' Companion to the Bible* developed a "Self-Inventory for Bible Readers" that we have adapted for working with youth.[12] In this self-inventory, we invite students individually to complete a worksheet of several questions designed to get them thinking about how their identities and cultures shape their assumptions about how to read the Bible. One set of questions asks students to consider how their attitudes toward the Bible have been shaped by their personal religious background and identity, including their relationship to a religious community, their family's religious background and views of the Bible, their current spiritual awareness and practice, and their life experiences. Another set of questions invites students to consider the standards and practices for approaching the Bible held by students' religious communities; the influence of preachers, teachers, and scholars they may have encountered; and their own "philosophy" regarding the Bible. Another set invites students to consider how their ethnicity, race, nationality, gender, and socioeconomic background might influence how they read the Bible. Another set invites students to consider how their political viewpoints and values—including the stance of being "nonpolitical"—influence their reading of the Bible. Yet another set invites them to consider the role of art, such as movies, music, plays, and other media, in shaping their views of the Bible.

Important to this exercise is emphasizing to youth that there are no "right" or "wrong" answers and that it is better to leave some answers blank than to make up answers that are not an accurate reflection of who they are and what they believe and think. Drawing a "blank" for a question is an opportunity to do further reflection, or even research, about one's history and culture. Also important to this exercise is a chance for students to discuss at least some of their answers with each other, ideally in small groups. The inventories could be completed and discussed in one session (about ninety minutes is needed) or completed at home and then brought to a meeting later to discuss in small groups, or the process could be spread out over two meetings. After the small groups have had at least twenty to thirty minutes to share from their inventories, the facilitator can then call the entire group together to debrief. If your youth group is part of a church that claims a historical connection to a founder (e.g., John Wesley, John Calvin, Martin Luther) or has an official stance on the Bible's authority, this is a great time to teach the students more about their own religious community's heritage. This large group time can also be a moment of "metareflection" on the exercise, exploring what questions were the most difficult to answer, examining what questions seemed more or less important to them in terms of shaping their views of the Bible, and brainstorming other questions that should be added to the inventory.

Most important, the facilitator should name explicitly the point of the activity: the purpose of this exercise is to encourage awareness of the role social location plays in biblical interpretation, both on oneself and on others. We seek to learn about ourselves and our relationships to the Bible because each person's perspective on what we are studying in the Bible has value and could be just the unique insight we all need to see something new or understand better what we are reading. We seek to learn about each other's relationships to the Bible because those different identities and life experiences mean that different people can come to different interpretations about a passage and still be "good faithful people" made in the image of God. We may not always agree, but listening to each other and taking each other seriously as fellow sojourners growing in faith is how we learn to build peace. By encouraging reflection on the role of identity and culture in shaping *how* we read the Bible, the facilitator (Beal's librarian) can help students understand why people of faith can come to disagree on *what* they read and invite students to ask questions based not only on their desire to understand the text more deeply but also on their desire to understand each other more deeply.

READING CACOPHONOUSLY *AND* INTERCULTURALLY: *HAVRUTA* STUDY

In Jewish education, the practice of *havruta* study engages students in reading both cacophonously and interculturally by bringing together a close study of sacred texts with intensive interpersonal engagement with a study partner. According to Orit Kent and Elie Holzer, the Aramaic term *havruta* means "friendship" or "companionship" and signifies the deeply social and collaborative nature of studying texts in pairs.[13] Simply put, havruta study involves two students reading aloud, slowly and repeatedly, a small segment of text, then working together to determine its meaning and then discussing their own views of this meaning. Kent notes that three pairs of "core practices" occur during this process: (1) listening and articulating, (2) wondering and focusing, and (3) supporting and challenging.[14] Through listening to the text and to each other, and articulating their different views of what they read, "*havruta* partners create space for each human partner and the text to be heard," and this "opens up room for new ideas to emerge and for shaping and refining ideas on the table." Through focusing closely on what is in a passage yet also wondering aloud about its implications and offering creative interpretations and applications of it, students take seriously the text on its own terms but also make meaning for themselves out of it. Through supporting one's partner by "providing encouragement for the ideas on the table and helping further shape them by clarifying them, strengthening them with further evidence, and/or sometimes extending them," and through challenging one's partner by "raising problems with ideas on the table, questioning what's missing from them, and drawing attention to contradictions and opposing ideas," students learn how to collaborate *even when they disagree* with the text or with each other and discover that they depend on each other to grow in wisdom.[15] Several researchers have noted that "*havruta*-style study" can be used with middle school, high school, and college students and can improve students' ability "to see multiple perspectives, appreciate the perspectives of others and use evidence to justify their interpretation," help them gain skills in discussing ideas with which they disagree as well as questioning sacred texts, and facilitate a sense of "accountability and interdependence" with other people as colearners.[16]

Havruta-style study could be adapted for a church Bible study context, and my suggestions for doing so draw on the research and refined practices of Kent and Holzer.[17] Begin by assigning students into pairs (or perhaps groups of three). The facilitator should assign the pairs, matching students who are at similar levels of literacy and experience with reading texts so that one partner does not dominate the other too much and to avoid someone feeling excluded by not being picked. Best friends should probably be separated, and attention to gender and personality dynamics is important.[18] The pairs should sit across from each other over a table if possible so that they can rest the Bible or the handout on the table and have their hands free to take notes and gesture. Give everyone the same passage, and keep it short—something that fits on one page of a handout or is no more than one Bible chapter (or shorter). Consider carefully the genre of the passage: narratives from the Old Testament, the Gospels, and Acts lend themselves well to creative exploration of the viewpoints of different characters; Jesus's parables are often difficult puzzles that lend themselves to multiple interpretations; proverbs often contradict each other or draw on everyday life in ways that lend themselves to hearty debates based on lived experience. Have available Bible dictionaries, Bible maps, concordances, multiple translations (e.g., NRSV, NIV, CEB, etc.), and if possible, photocopies of pages from a variety of commentaries on the selected passage so that students can begin to see different ways that the same passage has been interpreted. Have students take turns reading the passage out loud to each other, multiple times, and slowly. Encourage them to try to answer fact-based questions on their own by looking them up in the resources or asking you as you move around the room.

After gathering data together, students can take turns trying to articulate their interpretations of the text. When student A articulates her interpretation, student B listens carefully and asks questions to clarify what she is saying. Student B can then look for additional support for student A's interpretation by pointing to evidence in the text or to other sources that would support this reading. Student B should also raise questions about the interpretation, pointing to evidence in the text that might contradict student A's interpretation or to assumptions student A has made that are not actually supported by the text. The goal is for student B to help student A come up with the strongest case for her interpretation of the text, regardless of whether student B agrees with that interpretation. For that reason, challenges should focus on the text and the ideas generated, never on the student herself. Student B then articulates his interpretation, with student A asking questions of clarification, offering support by finding evidence in the text or other sources to support this reading, and noting weaknesses or counterexamples to the interpretation as appropriate.

While this may be awkward at first, engaging in the practice regularly, particularly with the same partner over time, will make it easier. Name the fact that it may be hard sometimes to challenge people's interpretations and the Bible itself but that it is possible to do so in respectful ways for the purpose of everyone learning more together. Keeping everyone in the same room working together will make things noisy, but this "cacophonous hymn to God" can excite students and make it a little less awkward as they learn to work with each other and become less dependent on you as the facilitator.

By drawing on a traditional Jewish practice of paired text study, we can introduce students to a way of reading the Bible that more accurately represents the way the Bible reads itself and the way Jesus, Philip, and the Ethiopian read their Scriptures—as a diverse array of voices supporting and challenging each other across different moments of time, space, and culture.

FOLLOWING THE SPIRIT TO THE DESERT ROAD—AND BEYOND

John Paul Cooke, Lauren's partner in ministry and in life, has been known to say, "The safest and riskiest move is to hug the text as closely as possible" in youth ministry. Safest because most youth groups already engage in Bible study, and simple changes such as moving to a question-asking method can appear innocuous from the outside. Riskiest because once students really begin to engage the Bible in all of its messiness and each other in all their diversity, adults may not be able to control how youth consequently respond to the Spirit. The Ethiopian's immediate reaction to his text study was to ask Philip, "What would keep me from being baptized?" (Acts 8:36). As the implications of the Isaiah passage began to dawn on him, he looked out from his carriage, saw water, and knew he had to act. Led by the Spirit, Philip knew he had to act too, and in so doing, he radically changed the Jesus-following community to include people of all races, nationalities, gender orientations, and power positions.

As leaders trying new ways to teach peace through Bible study, we are embarking on what might feel like a "desert" or "desolate" road, running up to a strange carriage and hopping in to engage in some difficult questions. The greatest challenge for many of us is to move past the images of youth as incomplete adults and precocious delinquents so as to trust enough in young people and in the Holy Spirit to allow the time and space necessary for these shifts to produce fruit. The greatest challenge after that will be to welcome the fruit that comes, even if it pushes us to radical action. The risk, however, will be worth it.

Chapter Five
DOING MISSION INTERSECTIONALLY

The Youth Theological Initiative (YTI) scholars are moving about a large, open classroom. They move quickly from one side of the room to another, stopping at tables representing different governmental or corporate services—the education department, an employment office, the bank, the housing office, and the marketplace for furniture, clothing, and cars. They engage with the bureaucrats working at each office, roles played by various adults. Some scholars move smoothly through the process, stopping first at the education office to gain a college degree, then on to the employment office to obtain a job, and then to the housing office to find a place to live. Others stand in long lines or sit in waiting areas, filling out long and confusing forms or waiting, bored, for a bureaucrat to call them forward. Others are told they do not have the money or the right degree or the right income to be able to get what they want at that station and are sent to another office.

There are other stations in the room. One is a church with a food pantry. Another is the city park, in the center of the room. Yet another is the county jail, with a courtroom adjacent to it. A few scholars wander aimlessly, unable to visit any of the bureaucratic offices. They stop at the church to ask for food or to sit and pray, or they sit in the park to rest and figure out what to do. Often, the police officers will come through the park and take to jail any participants who linger there too long. In jail, they join the others awaiting their trial in the courtroom, watching from the sidelines as the rest of their peers continue to play the game.

Just at the moment when some scholars become visibly frustrated, we call time. We've just played the "Game of Life."[1]

The Game of Life is an elaborate simulation of structural oppression.[2] Scholars are assigned various identities—generally quite different from the ones they have in "real life"—that include class, race, immigrant status, sexual orientation, disability, and gender identity. Scholars do not know what combination of identities they carry with them into the game; they are simply given different amounts of play money and told to "go out and live."

They quickly discover, however, that the game of life is harder to play for some than for others. The adults playing the role of bureaucrats—bank tellers, government workers, salespeople, police officers, and court judges—are instructed to use "microaggressions" to treat scholars differently based on the social location code on their name tags.[3] Those scholars coded as "poor" the adults repeatedly ask to go to the end of the line at the housing office, escort out of the store, harass, or offer cans of food at the church. Those coded as "wealthy" the adults treat with deference and invite to jump to the front of the line—unless they are also coded as a person of color, in which case they might question them about the source of their income or praise them as an exceptional credit to their group. Those coded as "immigrant" they give forms written in gibberish, address loudly and slowly, and treat as though unintelligent. Those coded as "LGBTQIA+" they encourage to seek jobs as hairdressers or gym teachers and make unwelcome at the church. Those coded as "disabled" they ignore, speak to as if they are children, or discourage from attending school or securing a job. Though it is only a game, all participants—both adults and youth—become caught up in it quickly. Within thirty minutes of our simulation, real emotions are flying.

This is just one way we try to prepare youth to practice mission and service as peace builders and justice seekers.[4]

JESUS AND THE DISCIPLES GO ON A SHORT-TERM MISSION TRIP

Both Matthew and Mark include a story about Jesus that most of us would rather not think about too hard. In Mark, it is Jesus's encounter with the Syrophoenician woman, an immigrant Greek speaker (Mark 7:24–30). In Matthew, Jesus encounters a Canaanite woman (Matt 15:21–28). We all know her as the "dog woman," however, because, quite disturbingly, Jesus calls her a dog when she asks him to heal her daughter. Most biblical scholars believe that Mark's Gospel was written before Matthew and Luke and thus assume that Matthew knew of Mark's version but made some slight yet significant changes to it. Both versions yield important insights for us about doing mission with youth, but we will focus on Matthew's version because his changes seem to raise the stakes even higher.

For much of Matthew's Gospel, Jesus has been using the Galilee region as a base for his ministry of teaching and healing. He picks up his first disciples by walking along the sea (Matt 4:18); he travels throughout this region to teach in the synagogues (4:23), delivers his Sermon on the Mount in this area (5:3–7:29), and teaches the crowds while standing on the seashore (13:1–52). Along the way, he heals many people, and though he is always on the move, that movement is in the general region of Galilee—that is, until he decides to take the disciples on a short-term mission trip to the regions of Tyre and Sidon. Further northwest of Galilee, the regions of Tyre and Sidon were part of the province of Syria and outside the political boundaries of Herod's kingdom. To go there, Jesus and his disciples not only left their main base of operations; they left their country. They are in foreign territory.

Once inside this foreign territory, a woman from that region, described by Matthew as Canaanite, comes out and shouts at Jesus and his mission team. She asks Jesus, whom she calls "Son of David," to show her "mercy" because her daughter is suffering terribly from demon possession. Jesus does not respond to her. Nevertheless, she persists. The disciples, disturbed and annoyed by her shouting, "urge" Jesus to send her away. And, it seems, Jesus attempts to do this. He tells her, "I've been sent only to the lost sheep, the people of Israel." Switching tactics, the woman stops shouting and running after the group and instead kneels before Jesus and calls him "Lord," now begging him to help her. Even after this groveling, Jesus appears to humiliate her further by responding, "It is not good to take the children's bread and toss it to dogs." Taking this insult, the woman says, "Yes, Lord." And tries one more tactic. Using the insult to her advantage, she reminds Jesus that "even the dogs eat the crumbs that fall off their masters' table." This apparently does the trick, and she gets what she wants. Her daughter is healed instantly (Matt 15:22–28). While in Mark's version it is the woman's clever response that Jesus declares to have changed his mind (in Mark 7:29), in Matthew's version, Jesus points to her "great faith" as the reason for his change in policy (Matt 15:28).

Matthew and Mark indicate that after this incident, Jesus leaves this foreign region and heads back to his home base in Galilee, leaving us confused and disturbed and with many unanswered questions. Why did Jesus want to go to this foreign territory in the first place if his intent was not to engage with the local people? On the other hand, if Jesus did intend to heal a local woman on her own soil, why did he engage her in such a domineering way? Did Jesus change his mind in this moment, or did he actually know in advance what was going to happen but wanted to show the disciples (or did Matthew want to show his readers) how to change their minds in order to expand the mission to the gentiles? Whether he truly believed the woman to be a "dog" or just acted that way in order to teach others how to move beyond that ugly prejudice, Jesus seems to be using this woman for the benefit of our learning and spiritual growth. This is really disturbing.

It is no wonder that most interpreters of this story overlook this disturbing implication—it challenges our image of Jesus as perfect and loving. Rather than ask questions about why Jesus behaved as he did, we typically focus on the woman and the final result:

because she made herself worthy, she received healing. Often, we romanticize this woman as a model of faith (or perhaps cleverness, if we follow the Markan version). And, certainly, her faith and her cleverness are qualities to admire. But when we focus on this story as a pivotal point in the origins of Christian mission—the moment in which people from foreign lands become the target for missionary work in the name of Jesus—dangerous problems arise.[5] While Christian understanding of mission and service usually looks to Matthew 25:31–46 (the judgment of nations in which those who gave food to the hungry, drink to the thirsty, and clothing to the naked are welcomed into the kin[g]dom, while those who did not are sent to eternal punishment) and Matthew 28:16–29 (the commissioning of disciples to "go and make disciples of all nations") as foundational, it is from the Canaanite woman's story that we must first learn if we want to do mission with young people in ways that overcome silence and transform violence.

MISSION TRIPS AND SERVICE PROJECTS: THE GOOD, THE BAD, AND THE UGLY

While the church has always been engaged in mission, the rise of the short-term mission trip, especially as a central feature of youth ministry for middle-class and predominantly white congregations, is a more recent innovation, as air travel became more accessible and a globalized economy connected us to each other more explicitly. Mission trips can be "urban plunges" into one's own city, van trips to areas of the United States hit by natural disasters, or long-haul flights to the Holy Land, sub-Saharan Africa, or eastern Europe. They can include a range of activities, including worshipping with local congregations, providing building materials and labor, leading activities with children, visiting pilgrimage destinations, or learning about community challenges from local leaders. They can last a weekend, a week during spring break, or even most of the summer, with agencies ready (for a fee) to arrange it all for us. By the time the National Study of Youth and

Religion (NSYR) began its nationwide, longitudinal study of young people and their religious practices and beliefs in 2002, service projects and short-term mission trips emerged as common facets of the religious experience of many of the youth they studied.[6]

At the same time that mission trips became easier and more popular, K–12 schools and colleges and universities began to see the value of including community service as part of the curriculum—what is now called "service learning." Schools began hiring directors of service learning, community service, or community partnerships and urging teachers to create assignments connected to course material that required students to go out into the community. Though implemented in a wide range of ways, service-learning activities must at minimum include students engaging in "activities that address human and community needs" along with "structured opportunities intentionally designed to promote student learning and development."[7] At their best, service-learning activities give equal weight to advancing effective learning while engaging in work that makes a lasting, positive impact on the community. In an effort to achieve this goal, the field of "service learning" arose, and scholars began to research the impact of doing community work as part of formal learning.

The research on both short-term mission trips and service-learning activities paints a complicated and often disturbing picture. On the one hand, several studies indicate that engaging in short-term mission and service-learning projects teaches young people to be better citizens and better Christians. Such engagement develops kindness and habits of service to others, helps youth feel more bonded to their church, helps youth develop a meaningful faith life, and increases young people's civic engagement once they return to their own communities. It can help young people recognize what it means to live out a Christian vocation in the rest of their lives and can have a profound effect on their views of God and God's nature, deepening their religious belief and practice afterward.[8]

On the other hand, seasoned teachers and pastors have raised several criticisms of the impact of mission trips and service projects on the communities and the students themselves. These projects are often shaped by a middle-class, white perspective that ignores the race, class, and gender dynamics within the group engaging in the service, as well as the dynamics between the servers and the served. In some cases, such trips and projects actually reinforce racist and classist stereotypes. International mission trips and service projects can devolve into "poverty tourism" or provide a series of experiences or exotic images for visitors to consume, turning local people into romanticized objects of pity or inspiration, and lead to new forms of colonialism and dependency.[9] Several human relief agencies cite specific harm that comes from short-term volunteer programs in orphanages, which traumatize children whose hearts break every time an adult in their lives connects with them and then leaves, and medical mission trips, where unqualified volunteers offer medical services they are not trained to do.[10] The carbon footprint of international flights—in which, for example, a round-trip transatlantic flight emits enough carbon pollution to melt about three square meters of sea ice—not just threatens "the stability of the earth's climate" but also causes "climate disruption on the very peoples and places that our work seeks to illuminate."[11] The amount of money spent per person to travel on international mission trips (some estimate at least $1,000–$3,000 per person)[12] makes it difficult for youth and churches with limited means to participate and could more effectively be given directly to those communities in need to hire local labor and thus contribute to local economic development.

All of this can result in teaching terrible lessons to our students while inflicting real harm on the persons being "served." The harmful lessons we may be teaching youth include the following: that individual suffering is the result solely of individual choices; that Christians are only called to tend to the wounds of injustice rather than to name and transform the larger unjust forces that hold us all in bondage; that recipients of our service have nothing of value to contribute to their own flourishing; that middle-class, suburban white communities are superior to communities of color and rural or urban communities; and that American culture is superior to cultures in other countries. If we want to engage in the kind of service and mission work that overcomes silence and transforms violence, we need to take seriously what the Canaanite woman has to teach us.

LESSON ONE

Before venturing into unfamiliar territory, study its history and how your history intersects with it. The details of both Mark's and Matthew's versions of the story matter. Mark makes a point of describing the woman as "Greek, Syrophoenician by birth" (Mark 7:26), a woman who is in the region as an immigrant. This marks her clearly as an outsider, but one whom early Christian readers would recognize from their current social context (more on this below). Matthew, however, makes an odd editorial choice by describing her as a Canaanite. By Matthew's time, this term had fallen out of use, so we can only conclude that Matthew uses it to conjure up some of the darkest aspects of Israelite history. From Genesis through Joshua into Ezra-Nehemiah, the Canaanites often symbolized what was unclean, dangerous, and detestable for Abraham and his descendants. The Canaanites were among the tribes of Indigenous people living on the land later forcibly taken by Joshua and the Israelites during the conquest (see Joshua and Judges). Abraham and Isaac both explicitly state that they do not want their sons to marry Canaanite women (Gen 24:3; 28:1, 8). During the conquest, the Israelites were supposed to eliminate the Canaanites completely (Josh 3:10), but they were unsuccessful in this genocidal task and instead forced the Canaanites into slavery (Josh 16:10; 17:13). Yet, despite this unequal relationship, the Israelites and Canaanites continued to intermarry, and this becomes so detestable to the priest Ezra that he tears his clothes, pulls his hair out of his head and beard, and sits in shock for hours (Ezra 9:1–4).

Like a terrifying ghost, Matthew now conjures up the Canaanite woman, a reminder of the genocide and slavery the Israelites committed and a hated source of ritual impurity and seductive idolatry. The encounter in Matthew is one between descendants of conquerors and a descendent of the conquered, with both now living under Roman occupation. To know the history of the region is to know that the land is soaked with the blood of people fighting for control of it and that the different peoples in the land have had different experiences of power and justice living on it. The present moment of encounter does not happen in a vacuum but rather waits to see how participants will act in light of that history.

Practitioners of service and mission who take seriously the task of transforming violence advocate for a serious study of a context's history before venturing into it to serve. To this end, Eric Hartman, along with several other global service-learning professionals, has developed a set of ethical guidelines called "Fair Trade Learning" or "Community-Based Global Learning."[13] These guidelines include an expectation that "students . . . acquire a working knowledge of the host country's political history and its relationship to global trends and pressures, current events, group customs and household patterns."[14] Tania Mitchell distinguishes "critical service-learning" from "traditional service-learning" by its willingness to encourage students to "examine both the historical precedents of the social problems addressed in their service placements and the impact of their personal action/inaction in maintaining and transforming those problems."[15] Before heading to Mexico, visitors from the United States should study the history of how Manifest Destiny affected the Mexicans living on the land we now call Texas, California, New Mexico, and Arizona. Before heading to Costa Rica, Haiti, or Bolivia, they should study the history of US policy in Latin America. Before traveling to the Democratic Republic of the Congo or Zimbabwe or South Africa, US visitors need to understand the history of Western colonialism and the different roles that Western Christian missionaries played in this history. Before going "into the city," visitors from the suburbs or from wealthier parts of the city need to understand the history of urban planning and the role that race and class have played in determining where people live and the quality of services available in those neighborhoods. Before going into the mountains or to rural areas, visitors from cities and suburbs need to learn the history of globalization and its impact on agricultural and mining practices. And as we learn these histories, we must ask ourselves, What role have our predecessors played in creating the situation that we now encounter? Who were—or still are—considered the Canaanites in this situation?

At YTI, we have found several practices useful in preparing our scholars for mission and service by learning history. High-quality documentary films that provide engaging overviews of historical and current events, or feature films and young adult novels that show the impact of those histories on particular characters, coupled with reflection and group discussion, have helped us dig into the impact of mass incarceration on communities of color, mountaintop removal on Appalachian communities, colonization and enslavement on Latin American and African peoples, immigration policy on Latinx and refugee communities, and dispossession from the land on Native peoples in North America. When possible, we have visited with leaders from the communities before engaging in work, sometimes taking a walking tour with them, in order to learn about this context from someone deeply familiar with it.

A particular practice we have used to begin the process of asking questions about the history of places we visit is an exercise called "Mapping Your Hometown." A simple internet search will lead you to find examples of "judgmental maps" for a number of cities, a phenomenon that inspired this exercise. Judgmental maps are both humorous and offensive because they label the different parts of a city or area based on stereotypes about the residents. While I don't recommend sharing too many of these maps in the middle of a youth gathering (many include curse words and are brutally direct about the race and class stereotypes that people hold about their fellow residents), these maps, in their directness, speak a truth about how power and privilege become visible in where and how we live and reveal local knowledge. In the "Mapping Your Hometown" exercise, I ask scholars to draw maps of their own communities, following a set of instructions that ask them to locate on their maps the realities of community divisions and disparities of resources: Where are the wealthy neighborhoods? Where are the poor ones? Where do immigrants or refugees live? Where do families, singles, students, and senior citizens live? Where do different races and cultures live? Where is the landfill located? Where are the nice parks? When tourists come to town, where do they go? What areas are considered dirty or dangerous? What are considered pretty or safe? Where are the important decisions made about what happens in the area? Who makes those decisions? Where do they live?

I then ask each scholar to mark on the map where they live, where they go to school, and where they spend most of their time. As we share our maps with each other, we begin to think about larger histories and forces that have influenced where and how people live. In a group that might come from the same area, differences in experiences with these dynamics become apparent. In a group that comes from different areas, we can compare how similar dynamics of division and concentration of power manifest themselves in every place, even if the specifics look different in each case. By developing an awareness of our own familiar communities, we prepare ourselves to look for the same dynamics when we enter other ones and become aware of the deep histories that will shape our encounters with the communities we hope to serve.

LESSON TWO

The complexity of our identities and histories shapes the ways we engage in service. Thus we must engage in intersectional self-awareness. Sometimes we forget how truly radical it is that we worship a God who chose to become incarnate in a human body. Jesus of Nazareth was a particular human being in a particular body born into a particular place and time. There are no "generic human beings," and there is no generic Jesus. Our Scriptures reveal to us that the Word made flesh inhabited a body identified as male, practiced the Jewish faith, came from the line of King David, lived in a region under Roman military occupation, and traversed an area marked by divisions among religious sects, tribal affiliations, wealth, and access to power. This complex set of identities that Jesus holds plays out in all of his interactions but in a striking way with the Canaanite woman, who was different from him in almost every way. Her people have been dispossessed and enslaved, and she is marginalized further because of her gender identity. She is not the first gentile he heals, but she is the only gentile he demeans. In Matthew 8:5–13, Jesus heals the servant of a Roman centurion—presumably someone involved in the military occupation of his people—without any resistance and is impressed by the centurion's understanding of power and hierarchy, even as that hierarchy is being used to further the power of Caesar. Jesus's interaction with a Roman male with immense power is very different from his interaction with a Canaanite woman with little power. In the second interaction, Jesus's identity affords him much more privilege and power than in the first.[16]

Understanding why and how this dynamic works is the basis for the concept of intersectionality. Originally coined by legal scholar Kimberlé Crenshaw in 1989, the term has become increasingly important for naming the complex ways that race, class, gender, and other identities "intersect" with and overlap with one another, making the unique mix of identities and histories of one person different from another, with some identities affording more power and privilege than others, depending on the context.[17] Understanding intersectionality, and how it operates in and through our engagements with people coming from different contexts, is critical to engaging mission and service in ways that overcome silence and transform violence. Tania Mitchell notes that a critical service-learning pedagogy—teaching social justice through community engagement—"asks everyone to approach the service-learning relationship with authenticity," which includes acknowledging "the power relations implicit in our interactions" and recognizing "the complexity of identity." She recommends that students engage in conversations about their "identity, personal histories, and experiences of privilege and oppression" in the classroom and suggests "experiential activities, simulation exercises, and personal reflection" to "facilitate self-awareness exploration." Such exploration can help students create relationships with those they encounter, relationships "that neither ignore the realities of social inequality in our society nor attempt to artificially homogenize all people in the service-learning experience."[18]

At YTI, we use several different exercises to facilitate this kind of exploration. In the Game of Life simulation exercise described at the beginning of the chapter, we show scholars how intersectionality works by giving them a complex set of identities under which to operate while playing the game. As much as possible, we try to assign identities that are different from the actual identities of our youth, both to make it more difficult for them to guess their identities right away and to encourage youth to step into the shoes, however briefly and artificially, of someone different from themselves. In the reflection after the game, scholars add up their net worth, and we group them by economic class to compare notes. Within each group, results differ because scholars' complex identities, including their race, immigration status, and gender and sexual orientations, affect how well they can navigate the system. Because of the multiple layers of their assigned identities, the same scholar might experience respect or warmth in certain spaces yet be treated with suspicion or condescension in others. This helps us show how the intersections of our identities affect us differently depending on context.

We also use an exercise called "Who Am I?," in which scholars list out all the ways they choose to complete the phrase "I am a(n) _____." Scholars list many things: they are siblings or only children, they are athletes or actors or dancers, they are Christians or agnostics, they are children or grandchildren, they are Black or one and a half generation Korean American or Ethiopian, they are southerners or midwesterners, they are male or female or nonbinary, they are conservative or liberal or apolitical, they are nature lovers or cat people or dog people.

As they review their list, we ask them to consider the following questions:

Think about a place where you spend a lot of your time (school, church, sports practice, work, etc.). Pick *one* of these places, then go back through your list and circle all the aspects of who you are that you feel you can show or be proud of in that space. What do you notice about which aspects of your identity you circled or did not circle?

Think about the place you most enjoy spending time. It might be the same place you named above or a different one. In the place where you most enjoy spending your time, how much of who you are can you show or be proud of? What makes this place enjoyable for you?

Are there spaces where you feel you have more influence, are taken seriously, can make some decisions for yourself, or can contribute your ideas?

Such questions encourage reflection on where someone might be on the margins and where they might be closer to the center, where they might have some power (perhaps more than they realize or acknowledge), and where they feel they have little power. In our group discussion, we talk about how our complex identities intersect in different ways, in different contexts, and in response to different people and that in all of this, we can find places where we do have power and can choose to use it wisely.

LESSON THREE

Even the most faithful Jesus followers have some unlearning to do when we engage in service. In Matthew's version of the story, the disciples are witnesses to the exchange between Jesus and the Canaanite woman. In fact, they instigate it. Presumably irritated by her incessant shouting, they come up to Jesus and urge him to send her away. His first response falls in line with exactly what they assumed would happen and no doubt thought appropriate: Jesus tells her that he has been sent "only to the lost sheep, the people of Israel" (Matt 15:24). This is precisely what Jesus told them to say when he commissioned them to engage in mission in 10:5. Jesus taught the disciples a particular theology of mission, a theology that made clear the differences between them and others and established an order of priority for who is "worthy" of the disciples' services. Of course the woman should be sent away; according to all that Jesus had taught the disciples, she was not worthy of their mission.

Even the most faithful of Jesus's followers can bring attitudes with them that cause harm when they engage in mission and service—attitudes they may even believe are justified by Jesus's own teachings. How often have we heard arguments against addressing poverty because Jesus said we will "always have the poor with [us]" (Matt 26:11)? Or explanations that people are homeless because they are lazy, drunken, or on drugs? While it may seem obviously unjust to blame victims for their own suffering, those of us who have grown up in the United States have been bombarded with messages that proclaim the importance of rugged individualism and insist that we live in a meritocracy, in which those who work hard will invariably get ahead, while those who fall behind did something to deserve it. What assumptions do we have about who is worthy of receiving our volunteer hours? Our money? Our compassion? How much have we been taught that those who are poor are so because of their own failings? How much have we been taught to distinguish between those who deserve our compassion and those whom we can safely bypass because they are too unclean or sinful? How much have we been taught that those who are "oppressed" should want to be liberated into the lifestyles we lead and should be grateful for our help?

Those urging us to go beyond patronizing charity to engage in justice-oriented service and mission insist that we must unlearn many assumptions we have about "people in need." Sam Marullo and Bob Edwards point out the dangers of service projects that do not engage in reflection about the larger social structures that have created the need in the first place. If students come away from a service project or mission trip still assuming that "the shortcomings of individuals in need" are the "sole cause of the problems that service-learning activities attempt to address," then "it is quite likely that they have missed entirely the social justice dimension of the problem."[19] In the case of a white, suburban youth group working at an urban soup kitchen in which primarily Brown and Black men have come for food, it is easy to leave in place, and even reinforce, lessons from our white supremacist culture that teach us that Black and Brown men are lazy, unskilled, or too addicted to drugs to want to work. While it is important to acknowledge that individuals and communities *have needs*, we must unlearn lessons that teach us to define people solely in terms of their neediness and to ignore the root causes of those needs by focusing solely on the individual actions that might have contributed to them becoming "needy."

The Game of Life is rigged. When the scholars come into the room, they must pick up the name tag with their name on it. The name tags have different colors, indicating their socioeconomic status. In addition to these color codes, some scholars have an additional letter added in the corner of the tag, referring to their status as an immigrant, person of color, or LGBTQIA+ or disabled person. The name tags come with a set amount of play money, and that amount differs based on the color of the tag. Once the game starts, typically all of the scholars go straight to the education office. They have been taught well that one must first obtain a good education in order to find a good job. But when they arrive, the differences become apparent. Those with gold and blue tags are rushed up to the front of the line, and they find they have enough money to pay for college. They pay, receive their degree, and are quickly on their way to the employment office in order to find a job. Others are sent to the back of the line or asked to take a number and fill out paperwork while they wait. Those with an I (for "immigrant") are given paperwork written in gibberish. Others fill out their forms but wait a long time for their number to be called. When they finally come to the desk, they find they do not have enough money for college and are turned away. They head to the employment office, where they find they do not have the education for a good job, so they take a low-paying job to earn the money they'll need to go to school later. As facilitator, I call "payday" after about ten minutes, and those who have a job can go to the bank to receive additional money. Those who are waiting in an agency line during payday may have to give up their spot to go to the bank. Those who do not have a job look on, frustrated that they cannot work their way out of their situation. Some go to the church for help, others beg money off their friends, and some sit it out in the park, until the police officers ask them to move on or arrest them for loitering. Those who are arrested are usually convicted by the judge—unless they can pay a bribe—and convicted felons receive a black sticker on their tag, making it even more difficult to find work or housing.

For those who start off ahead, the game is easy and fun. They amass more and more degrees, better jobs, and numerous cars, houses, and clothing. In their glee, they often do not see what is happening to those who started off behind them. It takes a while before they notice that their peers are not treated in the same way. Not until the end, when we count up our net worth and assess who went to jail and how often and for what reasons, do those at the top realize just how difficult the game of life was for others.

For those who start off the game behind, it is frustrating, even demoralizing. Some are sent to jail so many times, they give up and decide to sit out the rest of the game in jail rather than continue trying to plead for a justice they realize will not come. Some become creative: I have seen young women discussing their plan to find richer men to marry in order to get ahead, and I have also seen some scholars pool their resources to help one person get ahead in order to return to help others. Some become self-destructive—they try to rob the bank or steal from the store or break out of jail. Rarely, but sometimes, a few of them try to stage a nonviolent protest to advocate for justice, but they find that their wealthier peers are too afraid of being arrested (even by fake police officers in a game!) and losing their privileges to stand with them.

In the discussion afterward, we ask those who decided to steal or beg or protest or give up why they made these choices—particularly since those choices invariably cost them more net worth. We ask those who "won" the game, those with the largest net worth, how they managed to do so well and why others did not. Once people share about the different barriers they experienced and their efforts to overcome them, it becomes clear to all in the room that ending up in jail or in poverty has at least as much to do with how many barriers you had to overcome as it did with the personal choices you have made. Experiencing the catch-22 of not having the education to obtain a good job and never having a good enough job to earn the money to go to school helps scholars see that there are structures of oppression at work that go far beyond the individual character flaws and virtues of the individual players. The Game of Life is not a meritocracy and neither is the world in which we actually live. It's a hard lesson to learn, one that goes against much of what is taught in our schools, churches, and society, but it is a necessary lesson before heading out to help those "in need."

LESSON FOUR

We are enmeshed in principalities and powers that degrade us all, even Jesus. But Jesus also redeems those powers—and us. I have spent many hours with this biblical passage and have preached on it several times. More than anything, I want to find a way to avoid the conclusion that Jesus is acting like a jerk here. But the more I put myself in the place of the Canaanite woman, the more I cannot ignore the fact that *even if* Jesus set up this scenario in order to teach the disciples that it was time to change the mission and include the gentiles in the kin(g)dom, *even if* Jesus called her a dog in order to show us just how ugly it is for us to call anyone a dog, *even if* the woman started out by demanding that Jesus and the disciples recognize her humanity, *in the end the woman had to get on her knees to beg.* She had to play along with the dynamics of oppression in order to get what she needed for her daughter. Everyone in this story was degraded. Jesus was degraded by speaking an insult and wielding power over the woman; the woman (who has no name) was degraded by going to her knees after repeated attempts to maintain her dignity while asking for help. Does she use that moment of submission to turn things around? Yes. But it is in the fact that a relationship of domination and submission could not be eliminated, only leveraged, that we see how intransigent systems of oppression can be and how much they can bring out the worst in us, even when we want to do good.

Randy Stoecker is a sociologist who has studied and practiced service learning and civic engagement in higher education for many years. In *Liberating Service Learning and the Rest of Higher Education Civic Engagement*, Stoecker levels a devastating critique against some of the fundamental premises of the practice of service learning, a practice that many of our youth engage in through their schools and what we in the church emulate in the hopes of teaching them Christian witness and action. Stoecker begins by pointing out the historical association of "service" with noblesse oblige—that is, the supposed moral obligations of nobility to their subjects.[20] When we speak of being "blessed" and wanting to "give back," we are drawing on this model of assuming our role as people in power who perform virtuous acts using people with less power as our props. He then explains that in our current context, the primary way of distributing services and goods to people for free or below cost—food pantries, free clinics, after-school enrichment programs—is through 501(c)(3) organizations, institutions that operate with a business model that relies on volunteers, donors, and charitable foundations to cover costs. Tax-exempt institutions are severely limited by the tax code in their ability to participate in political advocacy. Additionally, they often must tailor their programs to fit the interests of the agencies that give them grants, interests that may or may not align with what the community really needs. This creates the "nonprofit industrial complex," a system that functions to provide "just enough charity to maintain the victims of an unjust social system while doing nothing to change that system," helping "keep the angers and resentments of the have-nots from boiling over while those with the most power and wealth continue to accrue more than their share of both."[21] Those on the receiving end of these services know the limits of these systems, and they adapt what they ask for and how they ask for it in order to get at least some of what they need. Seen from this perspective, our participation in service projects and short-term mission trips does very little to change the larger unjust systems within which we operate and forces those who serve and those who receive into set patterns that can dehumanize everyone.

In addition to exploring the concept of intersectionality, we at YTI use our reflective conversations after the Game of Life to explore the concept of structural oppression and how merely participating in the game can make us behave in ways that cause harm to others. The scholars who began the game with the most social and financial capital always amass more and are very rarely aware of the fact that their peers are struggling to keep up or play the game at all. The scholars at the bottom of the social hierarchy find themselves in and out of jail and unable to find work because of their criminal records and become genuinely angry or despondent. The adults playing the bureaucrats are amazed at how quickly they themselves take on the mentality of prejudice and suspicion and describe how seductive the abuse of power becomes. Resistance to the injustice is minimal, episodic, and confined to only a few people; on the whole, everyone assumes that the point of the game is to amass wealth and wield power as isolated individuals, and very rarely does anyone try to organize, share power or wealth, or stand in solidarity with others. Even when some participants decide to try to help each other out by sharing their resources, it never occurs to them to try to change the game itself.[22]

Christians have language for this, theological language that gets at the deepest root of this trap. We call these systems the "principalities and powers" (using KJV language), or simply the "powers." When the powers do this kind of harm, we call it (and them) evil. And when we participate in this harm—wittingly or unwittingly—we call it sin. In *The Powers That Be: Theology for a New Millennium*, scholar Walter Wink develops a biblical lens through which to recognize and understand the dynamics of structural oppression. Drawing primarily on the apostle Paul's use of the term *powers* (cf. Rom 8:38; Eph 3:10; 6:12; Col 1:16), Wink helps us see that the forces that cause violence and suffering in the world are not "up there" but "over there" and "in here"—that is, they are not separate heavenly bodies (i.e., Satan) but are the destructive spiritualities operating within the institutions and the people who participate in them (which is *all* of us). The powers are systems and institutions (bureaucracies, economic systems, governments, corporations, nonprofit agencies, schools, etc.) that were originally created good by God but have fallen to sin by turning their back on their divine vocation for the greater good in order to focus on narrow self-interests.[23] Evil thus encompasses more than just sinful actions by isolated individuals. It is corporate and systemic and "not simply the result of human actions, but the consequence of huge systems over which no individual has full control."[24] Thus even those organizations most committed to helping others often cannot escape participating in this larger system of economic injustice, racism, colonialism, and other forms of violence. The powers that are the nonprofit industrial complex and the big business of international volunteer tourism, on which we often rely for organizing our service projects and short-term mission trips, push us into roles of domination that can degrade us as well as the communities we visit. The fact that even Jesus has to contend with these powers means that our struggle is difficult and must be taken seriously.[25]

LESSON FIVE

Engaging in mission and service is disturbing, tests your faith, and challenges your assumptions, including your assumptions about Jesus. If it doesn't, you not only missed something critical; you probably caused more harm in the process. The story of Jesus and the Canaanite woman is very disturbing, especially if we sit with it and resist the urge to explain it away, downplay the harm being caused, or ignore the larger context of the story. Historically, interpreters of this passage have at times argued that Jesus called the woman a "puppy" as a sign of endearment rather than a dog.[26] Or they have romanticized the woman's subservient faith as a model of Christian virtue, ignoring the causes of her subservience. Some have doubled down on the righteousness of Jesus's exclusive focus on the house of Israel to remind us that *it is meant to be exceptional* for gentiles to join this mission.[27] But for those who want mission and service to "teach peace" with young people, we must push ourselves, and our youth, to sit humbly with the complexities and difficult implications of this story. Because this story is a pivotal moment for missiology, we must recognize that Christian mission—just like this story—is complex and difficult. We *should* be disturbed at the thought that we might be causing real harm in our well-meaning attempts to help others. We *should* stay awake at night wondering if our efforts to teach youth compassion, responsibility, and solidarity with those different from them might actually be reinforcing racism, colonialism, classism, and sexism.

We can face these challenges in two ways. First, we can make these concerns part of our conversation with youth before, during, and after we engage in service and mission. To turn traditional service learning into critical service learning, into a kind of service learning that has the potential for social change, Tania Mitchell insists that we must engage students in conversations that explore the root causes of the problems we observe in the communities we visit and we experience within our group as we visit them. We should ask,

> Why is service needed here in the first place?
> Why do we think we are able to contribute something positive to this situation?

> What can we learn from the people in this community about *their own* understanding of what is going on and how they are trying to address it?
> Does our work help address the root causes of the problems this community has identified?
> Why are there significant economic gaps between different countries or different racial groups or different regions?
> Why does the richest country on earth have such a serious problem with homelessness?
> Why is there such a big difference in the quality of services, such as schools, grocery stores, clinics, or banks, between different communities?

In other words, we have to ask big questions (the "Why?" questions) and destabilizing questions (the "Really? Are you sure?" questions). And when we arrive at the end of our knowledge, when we realize we don't really know why or we aren't really sure, we then do more research, asking people with local knowledge, so that we can get at root causes and overcome our misinformation and misguided assumptions.

Second, we can let the people with whom we engage change us. When Jesus finds Matthew sitting at a kiosk collecting taxes and calls him to follow him, Matthew responds immediately, no doubt grateful to be included as a disciple despite his participation in the oppressive system of taxation that supported the Roman Empire. The Pharisees' response underscores this, as they ask the disciples how Jesus could include Matthew and hang out with his fellow "tax collectors and sinners" (Matt 9:11). Jesus responds to the Pharisees, telling them that "healthy people don't need a doctor, but sick people do," and then challenges them to go back to Hosea and study their own Scriptures where it says, *"I want mercy and not sacrifice"* (Matt 9:12–13; Cf. Hos 6:6). When the Canaanite woman shouts at Jesus, she specifically shouts, "Show me mercy" (Matt 15:22), as though deliberately challenging Jesus to practice what he just finished preaching to the Pharisees.

The Canaanite woman reminded Jesus for what he stood. For the sake of the integrity of Jesus's teaching and mission, he had to change—and he does! Can we as leaders acknowledge when we need to change our minds and actions when confronted by those we think we are serving? Can we be transparent about this evolution so that even when we are exposed as hypocrites, we can make this a moment of transformative learning, not just for ourselves, but also for the youth who are watching us? For it was in watching Jesus change that the disciples themselves unlearned an unjust theology of mission and began to learn something far more radical.

The Canaanite woman is a specter Matthew conjures up, a ghost who haunts the consciousness of the readers and drives them to go deeper, to ask the harder questions, and to be brave enough to face the uncomfortable answers—and change our theologies and prejudices as a result. She teaches us that mission trips and service projects should do the same.

LESSON SIX

The work of mission and service is God's work of healing and restoration. Matthew's Gospel is a gospel of healing. The moment Jesus begins his ministry, he combines teaching and healing. People from throughout Syria hear about his healing power and bring to Galilee "all those who had various kinds of diseases, those in pain, those possessed by demons, those with epilepsy, and those who were paralyzed" (Matt 4:24). As he continues his teaching, crowds follow him everywhere, asking for healing (8–9). When Jesus commissions the Twelve for mission, he does so by giving them "authority over unclean spirits to throw them out and to heal every disease and every sickness" (10:1). Mission is about healing and restoration to wholeness in body, mind, and spirit.

Mission is also about the *Missio Dei*—that is, about *God's* movement in the world to bring about healing and restoration. Just as God the Father sent God the Son, Jesus Christ, into the world, and just as God the Father and God the Son send God the Holy Spirt into the world, so too does the Triune God send us into the world to participate in God's work of healing and restoration. Because it is God who sends us, we do not own or control this work.[28] We approach it with humility, fully aware of the potential for harm—to our youth as well as to those we try to serve—but we act in faith that God will show up if we see our work as God's, not our own. It is disturbing to watch the encounter between Jesus, the disciples, and the Canaanite woman. We cannot understand fully what this story means, nor can we fully understand how God works in the world. We only know that the daughter *was* healed, Jesus and the disciples *did* change, and this occurred because they encountered each other out in the world.

As problematic as short-term mission trips and service projects can be, Christians cannot conclude that they should not try to help others in need. Matthew 25:31–46 makes clear that our very inclusion in the kin(g)dom depends on our willingness to feed the hungry, offer a drink to the thirsty, welcome the stranger, clothe the naked, care for the sick, and visit those in prison, for when we do these things "for one of the least of these," we have done it for Jesus (v. 40). Moreover, Matthew 28:16–20 shows Jesus commissioning the disciples again—this time to "make disciples of all nations" (v. 19). Jesus has commissioned those of us who follow him not to stay at home and congratulate ourselves on our piety but to go out and do what we can to make lives better and bear witness to the good news.

We do this best, however, when we engage in service and mission with an awareness that we are participating in God's mission, a mission of healing. As hard as the exchange between Jesus and the Canaanite woman is, it does result in the healing of her daughter. As we celebrate the daughter's healing, and participate in activities that help heal communities from poverty, disease, and violence, we must also remember that the mother needs healing, too, and so do all those who witnessed her kneeling before Jesus. As we design our service projects and mission trips, we must ask ourselves if our efforts will not only heal the symptoms of oppression (the daughter) but also make some progress toward addressing the root causes of oppression (the disparity of power between the Canaanite woman and those from whom she is forced to beg). If we can work to address the larger context in which we engage in service and mission, we might encounter the healing of not only the daughter but also the mother. And ourselves.

Chapter Six
PRACTICING WORSHIP PROPHETICALLY

Having worked with the Youth Theological Initiative (YTI) since 1996, I have many powerful memories. Many of them are from worship. Worship at YTI is my favorite part—the moment at the end of long, challenging days of living together in diverse community and exploring difficult theological and ethical issues when we come together with each other and with God to breathe, sing, lament, laugh, dance, testify, reflect, listen, and reconnect. Because we are an ecumenical, international, and multiethnic program, worship is different every night. The scholars plan and lead the services, with support from staff. They bring all of who they are into the worship space: their many artistic and intellectual gifts and—more important—their hearts. As we become more bonded as a community, shy scholars step forward, and scholars who initially appeared to "have it all together" begin revealing their brokenness through reflections, poems, prayers, and homilies. By the end of our weeks together, we are One Body, regardless of denominational affiliation. Our final worship service includes extended time for testimonials, a celebration of Communion, and an anointing with oil to send everyone out into a world in desperate need of our peace-building and justice-seeking gifts.

A variety of images of YTI worship come to mind: Of three young men dancing with choreographed precision that unleashed their passion for God and momentarily liberated them from toxic masculinity. Of a young woman from a denomination that does not recognize the leadership of women leading a prayer, terrified that God might strike her down—and then joyously discovering that God did not. Of a young man, reluctant to be part of our community, struggling with anger and isolation, sitting near the altar painting in real time his response to the worship of his peers around him, praying the only way he could in that moment—through art. Of prayers given in Korean, German, Spanish, Arabic, Amharic, and English, each led by scholars sharing their cultures with each other. These are images of inclusion.

I have more images: Of a handful of scholars gathering just before room check in a dorm room transformed into a prayer chapel, using the *Book of Common Prayer* to practice compline. Of a variety of breads—some bitter, some sweet, some hearty—in stations around the sanctuary, with scholars and staff taking different pieces of bread to represent how they were feeling in that moment, sharing with each other in a modified love feast. Of the community sitting in rows facing each other monastic style, chanting Taizé songs and praying the Psalms. Of a choir of diverse faces leading us in old hymns and gospel songs. Of teenagers and young adults overcoming awkwardness to wash each other's feet. Of a handful of youth raiding the sacristy for white robes and processing into the sanctuary with large candles and crosses. All these are images of reclaiming our traditions.

I have yet more images: Of "High Church" people timidly, then more boldly, participating in the cadence of call and response as they engage their bodies in hearing the preached Word. Of "Low Church" people timidly, then more boldly, participating in the back-and-forth of antiphonal psalm reading. Of the community learning together the song "Siyahamba" and its roots in the antiapartheid movement in South Africa and processing up to the chapel "marching in the light of God." Of the choir singing John Lennon's "Imagine"—including the line "imagine no religion"—as a heartfelt prayer to God for transformation of the world. Of our scholars and staff visiting a mosque, some lining up for jumu'ah prayer, others respectfully drawing back to the wall to observe, with all experiencing the sacred moment when hundreds of people prostrate themselves before God in total silence. All these are images of expansion.

And yet more: Of a Black staff person leading a prayer of lament hours after hearing about yet another shooting of an unarmed Black man, demanding that God stop the violence and be present with God's people, as Brown and Black participants cried tears of anger and fear while the other participants silently bore witness and wrestled with the implications of these laments for themselves. Of all of us forming a large circle around the sanctuary, putting our arms on each other's shoulders, and singing "Lean on Me," affirming that we are, indeed, One Body. Of different worship leaders giving the same benediction at the end of every YTI service, inviting all to pass the peace, the sanctuary exploding with hugs and high fives and laughter and song as scholars and staff try to pass the peace to every single person. All these are images of full-bodied expressions of hearts connected to God and neighbor.

In more recent years, I've started collecting other images of worship: Of Patrisse Khan-Cullors, one of the cofounders of Black Lives Matter, leading groups in a benedictory prayer drawn from Assata Shakur's "Letter to the Movement": "It is our duty to fight for freedom. It is our duty to win. We must love each other and support each other. We have nothing to lose but our chains."[1] Of Bree Newsome quoting Psalm 27 and the Lord's Prayer as she scaled the flagpole in front of the South Carolina State Capitol to bring that state's Confederate-themed flag down after the shooting of nine Black parishioners at Mother Emanuel AME Church.[2] Of Jonathan Butler, a graduate student at the University of Missouri, praying with his pastors for discernment and then engaging in a hunger strike, sparking a campus-wide demand for changes that would address the racism against and exploitation of students on his campus.[3] Of Emma Gonzalez, senior at Marjory Stoneman Douglas High School in Parkland, Florida, standing before thousands of people, speaking for two minutes and then standing in silence for four minutes and twenty-six seconds, marking the amount of time it took for a gunman to kill seventeen of her classmates, bringing every person in the crowd with her into that unbearable silence of death.[4] Of "Momma Cat" Daniels, described as "matriarch, therapist, chef and friend to demonstrators," cooking and setting up Sunday feasts for hundreds of protestors in Ferguson.[5] Of Greta Thunberg, instigator of the global youth-led climate strikes, fasting from the devastating carbon footprint of air travel by insisting on journeying by boat and train to her many speaking events.[6] Of Protest Chaplain Brenna Lakeson recovering enough from the tear gas shot at her by Atlanta police to go back to the front of a protest line to lay hands on a group of women who had fallen on their knees to pray and lament.

I write this chapter during the summer of 2020. We are in the throes of a global pandemic, isolated from each other; terrified of losing our jobs, getting sick, or dying; and grieving our inability to gather physically for Sunday services, for weddings, for graduations, for the funerals of those whom this disease has claimed. We are also in the throes of the greatest civil unrest in the United States since 1968. This moment is in its truest sense apocalyptic. The word derives from the Greek word meaning "to unveil" or "to uncover," and we are all watching as the frailties of human bodies, leaders, and institutions are uncovered before us, as the world we once knew melts away, and as something new—terrifying and hopeful—is being revealed. During this time, other images of worship have emerged: Of people gathering around laptops to watch videos of their pastors reading Scripture, praying, and preaching sermons and church musicians on split screens making music from multiple locations. Of thousands of protestors taking a knee in the middle of city streets. Of missionaries from around the world coming together online to pray the Lord's Prayer in their native tongues to fortify themselves as they continue their work on the ground fighting the pandemic. Of nightly rituals of cheering from balconies for health care workers during shift changes and daily deliveries of food to hospitals and houses of senior citizens. Of car parades to celebrate birthdays and offer encouragement. Of laypeople lighting candles, leading prayers, and gathering bread and wine to their own tables, discovering ways to worship as households. Of mourners standing in silence for eight minutes and forty-six seconds, marking the length of time police officer Derek Chauvin had his knee on George Floyd's neck. This apocalyptic moment is revealing different sides of ourselves, our neighbors, our faith communities, our institutions, and our leaders. We are all worshipping in new ways.

These many images of worship—some ancient, some evolving in real time, some within church spaces, many outside of them, some individual, some corporate—have the power to shape our lives because they have the power to shape our imaginations. They point us toward what we are worshipping and teach us on a level deeper than words whom and what to love. Worship forms us, and if we want our youth and ourselves to be formed as peace builders and justice seekers, we must pay attention to this power.

JESUS THE GOOD JEWISH BOY

In chapter 3, we zoomed in on a particular moment in the life of Jesus—his time as a teenager, sitting in the temple, listening and questioning the religious scholars and elders—as a model for doing deliberative theology with young people. If we pull out to a wider frame, we can more fully appreciate the significance of this moment for all of Jesus's life and ministry. Jesus, particularly seen through the lens of Luke's Gospel, was a good Jewish boy, from birth to death. His parents had him circumcised on the eighth day and brought him to the temple to dedicate him to the Lord, engaging in ritual cleansing and offering sacrifices "in accordance with the Law from Moses" (Luke 2:21–24, 27). By the time we find Jesus in the temple at age twelve, he has already been coming to the Passover festival with his family every year. Raised faithfully in accordance with Jewish religious practice, Jesus "matured in wisdom and years" (2:52), and this formation continues into his public ministry as an adult, as he visits synagogues on the Sabbath "as he normally did" (4:16) to teach and heal (4:15; 4:44; 6:6; 13:10).

The corporate worship of temple and synagogue were central to Jesus's religious practice, but he also engages in individual practices, and these practices sustain and strengthen him throughout his ministry. Jesus regularly withdraws from his followers to pray (Luke 5:16; 6:12; 9:18), prays with the disciples (9:28), and spends significant time teaching the disciples about prayer, giving them words to use (11:1–4) and providing illustrations of good and bad prayer practices through his parables and stories (11:5–13; 18:1–14; 20:45–47). It is to prayer that Jesus turns on the eve of his passion (22:39–46), and in this moment, he models all that he has been teaching his followers about prayer: he steps away to pray privately in order to pour out his heart to God sincerely; he kneels down in humility before God; he is focused and intense, almost athletic in his praying, with sweat falling on the ground; he prays boldly and earnestly for what he wants—to have the cup of suffering taken away—but in the next breath submits in trust to God's will. This prayer strengthens him, and he emerges from his prayer prepared to endure betrayal, torture, and abandonment on his journey to the cross. All this is in direct contrast with the disciples, whom Jesus repeatedly told to pray but who did not, and when the crowd arrives to arrest him, the spiritually unprepared disciples engage in violence (22:50), deny knowing him (22:54–62), or retreat into the distance (23:49).

Just as prayer makes it possible for Jesus to sustain his ministry, even unto death, fasting makes it possible for Jesus to claim his identity as the Son of God and to resist the temptations of the devil that would turn him away from this identity. Returning from the Jordan River, baptized and consecrated as the Son of God, the Spirit leads Jesus into the wilderness, where he fasts for forty days. While it is obvious that the physical hunger from this makes it tempting to turn a stone into bread, we miss something important about the nature of fasting when we assume it made Jesus more rather than less vulnerable to temptation. Fasting clears one's head, brings one closer to those who cannot eat, and makes one aware of the body's deep interconnection with the soul and its total dependence upon its Creator. Fasting *prepared* Jesus to engage the devil. The three temptations the devil offers Jesus are all forms of power that humans worship: turning stones into bread represents the economic power that comes from controlling material goods, worshipping the devil in return for dominion over all the kingdoms of the earth represents the political power that comes from controlling institutions and governments, and testing God by jumping from the temple pinnacle to force angels to save Jesus represents the religious power that comes from claiming to control how God works in the world. Jesus can resist these forms of power *because* of his fasting, not in spite of it. He is keenly aware of his body and its needs, is in deepest connection to those from whose suffering in the world he has come to declare liberation, and knows upon whom he is absolutely dependent. The devil says to him, "If you are the Son of God" (Matt 4:3 NRSV), and Jesus not only confirms that he is God's Son but shows the devil, and us, what kind of Son he will be. As Son of God, he will not engage in powers of domination and control. He will instead engage in a power far more radical—the power of resistance with love as its logic. To do this, however, Jesus engages in regular practices of prayer, fasting, and public worship that ground and sustain his ministry. If we want to follow Jesus in this ministry, we must engage in these practices as well. We must be formed by our liturgy.

WE ARE WHAT WE LOVE: UNDERSTANDING THE FORMATIVE POWER OF LITURGY

In *Desiring the Kingdom: Worship, Worldview, and Cultural Formation*, James K. A. Smith urges Christian educators to take seriously the pedagogy of worship, not simply as one aspect of teaching the faith, but as the underlying approach to all Christian discipleship.[7] Any philosophy of teaching assumes a theory of how human beings learn, and according to Smith, when we mistakenly assume that human beings only learn through ideas, we mistakenly assume we can pass on the faith simply by telling people what to think or believe. The mistake of modern liberal Christianity has been its reductionistic focus on Enlightenment rationality and the overemphasis on the "person-as-thinker." The mistake of modern conservative Christianity has been its reductionistic focus on doctrinal adherence and the overemphasis on the "person-as-believer."[8] Both assume that humans think or believe their way into faith and underestimate the power of love and desire in pointing our hearts toward or away from God and the power of habits, rituals, and practices in forming our characters at a level deeper than the cognitive. We learn to love through the repeated practices of worship, and we become what we love. If we want to become the kind of people who love God, neighbor, and enemy, we need to take seriously our practices of worship—inside and outside the church walls.

Smith explains that "to be human is to be on a quest."[9] All of us, regardless of whether we are conscious of it, are striving toward a telos, or goal. We live toward this telos, not primarily because we think about it, but because we want it, we long for it, we desire it. We have a vision of "the good life," which goes beyond our personal wants and desires but embraces a vision of what society should look like too, and this vision doesn't so much convince us as it *allures* us. We follow it because we love it, because "we are first and foremost *lovers*," before we think about it, before we decide to believe it.[10] Our hearts—not the modern romantic notion of the heart but the ancient notion of *kardia*, our gut instincts that drive us—are like compasses that set the direction of our lives toward a particular pole. This operates without our having to think about it and shapes what we do daily.

What Paul, Aquinas, and Augustine understood that we have forgotten in the modern world is the power of habits and the role of virtue in shaping the direction of our lives. When Paul urges the Romans to "put on the Lord Jesus Christ" by clothing themselves in compassion, kindness, humility, gentleness, and patience (Rom 13:14 NRSV), he is talking about the process of taking on the good moral habits—virtues—that make someone a Christian. As the ancients understood, we do not become good people simply by deciding one day to change—although that moment might serve as the first step toward that goal. Rather, we become good people through a long process of imitating good role models and practicing virtuous actions repeatedly over time, until it becomes "second nature," something we can do without thinking about it. Becoming like Christ is a process of training our "moral muscles," and just as it takes practice to become a good pianist or baseball player, it takes practice to become a virtuous person oriented toward the good. It is *natural* for us to love. It takes *training and practice* to learn to love rightly. These practices form a "pedagogy of desire" that teaches us to desire God's *shalom*, the good life as God intended, the flourishing of all creation through life-giving relationships of justice and peace.[11]

For Smith, the focus on habits and rituals gives us a way to approach Christian education (and youth ministry) more effectively. If we understand that humans are fundamentally "liturgical animals" who become what they love through the habits and practices of worship, we can see more clearly the limitations of educational efforts that appeal only to minds and not to hearts. We can also now see the limitations of *not* appreciating the formative power of our habits and practices that pervade our daily lives and may not be oriented toward God's *shalom*. Smith suggests that we pay attention to the "meaning-laden, identity-forming practices that subtly shape us," daily routines and habits that are "automating our desire and action without our conscious recognition."[12] In particular, he urges us to consider the "cultural liturgies"—the meaning-laden, identity-forming practices in which we participate as part of the society in which we live—that serve as "rival modes of worship," teaching us to love rival visions of the good life.

Smith analyzes three specific cultural liturgies, both to model a form of "cultural exegesis" he encourages us to do and to underscore how pervasive and "misformative" these cultural liturgies are. He begins with the "liturgy of the mall." If one puts on a "liturgical lens" and walks into a mall, one begins to see how the mall trains our hearts in a particular direction. Many of us make regular "pilgrimages" to the mall, when we arrive at an immense cathedral that welcomes us in to escape from our humdrum lives and leads into various "chapels" with "icons" dressed in the latest fashions that inspire us to imitate them as moral exemplars. When we enter these chapels, we are greeted by ushers who welcome and guide us, and when we find our "holy objects," we bring them to the "altar," where the "priest" consummates our worship through the transaction of give-and-take. We leave with sacred "relics" that are "wrapped in the colors and symbols of the saints and the season."[13]

The liturgy of the mall is a liturgy that shapes our hearts, not our minds. It does not need to tell us what to think, for it grabs us on an affective level and uses the beautiful to teach us multiple lessons: (1) that we are imperfect as we are and need to shop in order to change these flaws, (2) that we should judge others along a competitive scale of beauty and wealth, (3) that we are what we buy and that shopping is "therapeutic" and will make us happy, and (4) that we can engage in these rituals of consumption guilt-free if we pretend that they are available to everyone and ignore the devastation of communities and ecosystems that results in unbridled growth, consumption, and waste.[14]

As a college professor, Smith has had ample opportunity to turn the liturgical lens onto the cultural liturgy of the university, and he finds similar misformations at play here. Smith reminds us that from the perspective of a typical residential undergraduate student, the university extends far beyond the classroom and includes dorms, stadiums, and frat houses, all of which engage in "unofficial liturgies" that might be more formative than the robed ceremonies of convocation and commencement, not to mention the classrooms. Rituals such as "Fresher Week" at the beginning of the year "baptize" new students into the community through an initiation that "often amounts to carefree social interaction lubricated by alcohol, cult-like devotion to the football team, and the solidification of social networks that will be instrumental and instrumentalized for the sake of personal benefit and gain."[15]

The ritual of Rush Week for fraternities and sororities takes this a step further and adds more training in social networking that belies its ideal of class distinctions and sensibilities. The stress of all-nighters and the frenetic pace of schoolwork and extracurricular activities push out any possibility of Sabbath rest and form young bodies for an economic system of competition and overtime work in pursuit of status and material gain.

The university, through all of these rhythms and rituals, does an excellent job of preparing young people for "the real world" by taking those incomplete adults and forming them into "productive, successful consumers who will be leaders in society."[16] Seen through this liturgical lens, both our regular habits of going to the mall and our "rites of passage" in sending young people off to college are unveiled as experiences that misform us away from a vision of love for God, earth, self, and neighbor and toward a vision of economic power: controlling the world by turning stones into bread.

Smith next examines the cultural liturgies of sacrificial violence, particularly in the "military-entertainment complex." While the mall's liturgies shape us into good consumers, nationalistic rituals intend to shape us into "good, loyal, productive citizens who, when called upon, are willing to make 'the ultimate sacrifice' for the good of the nation." While this might be easily seen in military parades and national holidays, Smith reminds us that smaller, more frequent practices can have a big impact: saying the Pledge of Allegiance in school each morning, which mimics the creedal professions of the church and asks us to give our loyalties to a flag; standing for the national anthem as the opening ritual for sports events, which "rehearses and renews the myth of national identity forged by blood sacrifice"; watching numerous television shows and movies that celebrate the violence of the good guys over the violence of the bad guys, or justify the violence of our country against individuals and nations who dare to oppose us.[17] One might also consider the recruitment ads for the armed forces, which seduce us with images of strength, honor, sacrifice, and glory for the nation.

These are not just forming us to love a particular nation-state over God's kin(g)dom: they are forming us to be a people willing to die—and kill—for that nation-state. By turning our hearts toward a vision of a human institution that prizes material prosperity through competition, individual freedom through noninterference, and domination of other peoples and nations through military might, our regular habits of the "military-entertainment complex" promise us dominion over the earth's kingdoms in return for worshipping the demonic forces of blood sacrifice.[18]

After demonstrating the ways in which cultural liturgies can misform us into lovers of material wealth and class status and of spectacular violence and dominance, Smith argues for a reclamation of Christian worship as the site for engaging in "counterformation." Christian education, which for Smith includes the ongoing formation of children, youth, and adults of all ages, should take seriously humans as "liturgical animals" and teach us how to direct our hearts to love rightly. Chapter 5 of *Desiring the Kingdom* engages in an extended exegesis of Christian worship, examining closely the vision of the kin(g)dom that is embodied in everything from the design and decor of the worship space, to the rhythms of the liturgical seasons, to the way we welcome people into the space and begin the service. He examines this vision as revealed in the specific actions of the weekly worship service (e.g., call to worship; congregational song; readings and sermon; confession and assurance of pardon; creed; prayers for intersessions and illuminations; offering; benediction and sending forth). He reminds us of the vision of God's *shalom* so central in baptism and Eucharist. In all of this, Smith models a theology of worship that appreciates the wisdom of liturgies and practices that have shaped Christians for centuries and calls our attention to the importance of every detail in how we plan and lead worship.

By engaging in the exegesis of Christian worship, Smith intimates that worship services that jettison these core practices, or engage them ham-handedly, will undercut the counterformative power of worship in the midst of cultural liturgies that seek always to allure us with rival visions of the good life. Worship that focuses on entertainment, on chasing the next trend in order to be relevant, will merely continue the formation of the liturgy of the mall.

While Smith does not name this specifically, I would extend his argument to suggest that worship that primarily serves as a site for social networking, or that sends messages implicitly or explicitly that certain groups of people are not welcome in the sanctuary or at the Eucharist table, also continues the misformation of the liturgy of the mall and the university. Worship that blurs the boundaries between the cross and the American flag, between praying for the wisdom and courage of national leaders and praying for the triumph of national leaders over their perceived enemies, between holy days and national holidays, between a Jesus who dies at the hands of state violence and a Jesus whose death has been co-opted by the state to inflict violence on others continues the misformation of the liturgy of the military-entertainment complex. The temptations of turning stones into bread or giving allegiance to a false god in exchange for dominion over nations are ever at our doorstep—even the doorstep of the church.[19]

So, too, is the temptation of testing God. As I write, religious communities around the world are scrambling to find ways to gather while under quarantine. The cruel irony of Smith's argument is that the regular gathering of the faithful *in person* is essential to becoming God's people, and yet to gather in person at this time is to endanger the lives of thousands, if not millions, of people. Those pastors who have decided to resist shelter-in-place directives in order to meet in person rather than finding creative ways to maintain connection and encourage laypeople to continue their spiritual practices at home, online, and over the phone are succumbing to Jesus's third temptation. When the devil brings Jesus to the pinnacle of the temple, he dares Jesus to endanger his life, to prove that God is with him and will protect him from harm, perverting the meaning of Psalm 91 as he quotes it. Jesus resists this temptation because it seeks to usurp God's power for misguided aims. As central as worship is for our formation, the use of worship in willful disregard to the safety and lives of others surely cannot be forming our hearts toward a vision of God's *shalom*.

We have a deep tradition of worship practices honed by the wisdom of the centuries, and these practices, once reclaimed and integrated into our lives, can form our hearts for God rather than for the market or the nation. However, Smith recognizes that attending church once a week is simply not enough counterformation in the face of all that misforms us the rest of the week. He thus advocates a kind of "monasticism" that engages in "wise abstention" from certain cultural liturgies while adding "habits of daily worship" that may include additional gatherings for worship, "practices of hospitality and Sabbath keeping, singing and forgiveness, simplicity and fasting," reading Scripture, prayer, service, discernment, and other ways of staying connected to God and neighbor throughout the week. In all of this, Smith argues that these practices, even when engaged in at home by oneself or with one's family, are never disconnected from the world. Our "household liturgies," as well as our communal worship, always culminate in a sending forth, out into the world, to bear witness to the divine *shalom* we were created to enjoy.[20]

James K. A. Smith's cultural liturgies project offers us a particular theory we can build upon in our own attempt to form peace builders and justice seekers for God's *shalom*. First, Smith advocates and models a technique of "cultural exegesis" that we can use with our youth to examine other cultural liturgies in their lives, particularly those that train their hearts toward violence or disempowerment or shape their images of themselves as incomplete adults and precocious delinquents. Second, Smith models a form of "liturgical exegesis" that we can apply to our own church and youth group worship practices, considering how effective or ineffective we may be in inspiring a vision of God's *shalom* rather than inadvertently embodying false visions of the good life. Third, Smith calls us to take seriously the riches of our Christian tradition as sources of deep wisdom for Christian discipleship and not to assume automatically that young people will find them boring or irrelevant, a call that pushes us to mine our tradition for the wisdom it can offer us in growing as peace builders and justice seekers. Fourth, we can take on Smith's challenge to engage in a new kind of "monasticism" that employs both "wise abstention" and daily habits of personal and small group practices that seek a counterformation to the cultural liturgies that silence young people and perpetuate violence against them and against the world. To this work, we now turn.

COUNTERFORMATIVE PRACTICES FOR PEACE BUILDERS AND JUSTICE SEEKERS

Throughout this book, I have suggested practices that can help young people overcome silence and transform violence: practices of building inclusive community with youth, practices of engaging different theological viewpoints in democratic and deliberative ways, practices of studying Scripture that lift up questions and hold space for paradox and disagreement, practices of engaging in mission trips and service projects that reduce violence and respect the dignity of all involved. Our turn here to worship—understood both as public gatherings as well as individual acts of prayer and fasting—merely underscores how important practices are for teaching peace and justice and reminds us that worship and spiritual practices undergird all the others. If we want to help youth cultivate a faith that overcomes silence and transforms violence, we must be intentional about how we train our hearts to love the justice and peace of God's *shalom* embodied in Jesus's own actions. To do that we must first help youth understand how liturgies inside and outside the church are forming them—and us.

Cultural Exegesis: Reading the Liturgies of Our Lives

Toward what telos are high schoolers being formed each weekday from August to June? How are our daily habits of using our phones and engaging in social media forming us? What do we make of the rites of passage when someone turns sixteen and can drive a car, turns eighteen and can vote or be drafted, turns twenty-one and can legally drink alcohol? Do Smith's observations about the liturgy of nationalism in sports events help us understand what is so threatening about Colin Kaepernick "taking a knee" during the national anthem? Can we understand in new ways what might be happening on the level of the heart rather than the mind in political rallies, protests, vigils, and marches?

In *Desiring the Kingdom,* Smith offers a specific set of questions to encourage individuals and groups to consider the impact of cultural liturgies on our formation and misformation—what he calls a "practices audit."[21] As a youth group, participants could reflect on some of these questions together, as well as at home on their own, returning to share later. Some questions encourage us to observe the details of our daily habits: "What does your time look like? What practices are you regularly immersed in each week? How much time is spent doing different sorts of activities?" Other questions encourage us to evaluate these habits to weigh which ones are meaning laden and identity forming: "What are some of the most significant habits and practices that really shape your action and attitude—what you think and what you do?" Asking youth to keep a log over the course of a week, noting what they do in some detail from the moment they wake up until they go to bed, can reveal significant insights into how much their lives may be shaped by sports or exercise; extracurricular activities; school; homework; spending time with family, pets, and friends; playing video games; shopping; following social media; texting and talking on the phone; and sleeping.[22] Simply estimating how much time is spent on different activities might reveal how we prioritize them—or how they have been prioritized for us. The group can then consider which of these practices are forming them into the kind of people they want to be and the kind of people who are citizens of the kin(g)dom of God.

Moving from personal reflection to understanding the role of cultural liturgies, the group can then consider in greater detail the liturgy of the high school, similar to Smith's exegesis of the liturgy of the mall and the university. Ask students to list the regular practices that happen each school day from the moment they get on the bus or set foot on the campus to the moment they get home:

> What do the architecture and decor of the buildings look like? Are they inviting and in good repair? Do they look like places for people to learn or like places for people to be watched or controlled, or both?
> Must they go through metal detectors or other security rituals before they can go to class?
> How do the adults (teachers, administrators, volunteers, school resource officers or security guards, lunch staff, housekeeping staff) treat them, and how do students respond?
> How much time do they have between classes, and is there enough time to take care of bodily needs and get to class during that time?
> Is there enough time for lunch, and what is available to eat?
> What is included in the morning announcements and rituals (e.g., Pledge of Allegiance, celebrations of sports wins, moment of silence or prayer)?
> Do they have a dress code?
> How often do they have standardized tests?
> How often are rules about drugs, weapons, and conduct reviewed?
> How often does the school engage in lockdown drills?
> Are students subjected to random searches?
> What annual events do they have (e.g., prom, dances, honors night, senior activities, etc.)?
> What school traditions do students enjoy?
> What traditions do they dread?
> How are their bodies placed in the classroom? (e.g. how often do they face forward and passively receive information from the teacher, and how often do they sit at tables or in circles and engage in discussion with their classmates? Can they move around the classroom, or venture outside?)

How much of their time at school is spent on learning,
how much on extracurriculars, and how much on social
interaction or play?

It may not be obvious at first that these various details might work together to have an impact on them, so it may take some additional questions to begin to see the high school as its own kind of liturgy:

What does it mean that the school schedule is structured in
such a way that you move from space to space every fifty
minutes, with only five minutes in between? What does that
train your body to do?
Why are you asked to say the Pledge of Allegiance each day?
What do you think this practice teaches you?
What implicit or explicit messages do you think are being sent
by the fact that there are random searches of your lockers,
or that you have to prepare for the possibility of an active
shooter in your school?
What kind of person do you think the school wants you to be?
What actions does your school do that tell you this?

Does the school see them as incomplete adults or precocious delinquents? Depending on the kind of school they attend, youth might observe that their schools want them to become "productive, successful consumers who will be leaders in society" or that their schools expect them to become criminals, teen parents, or dropouts. They might observe their schools teaching them how to adapt their thinking to perform well on tests or to think for themselves. These messages undoubtedly differ across race, class, and gender, differences important to note.[23]

Learning to read the cultural liturgies around us helps us and our youth become aware of how our hearts are taught to desire rival kingdoms. The liturgy of the high school is important to consider because it is the dominant cultural liturgy in which American youth engage and one that trains their hearts toward specific images of the society they are expected to join. Smith wants Christian worship to be central to the habits of those who want to learn to love God, and so he does not consider cultural liturgies that might form hearts in directions that could complement the counterformation that Christian worship provides. I believe we can expand his concept of cultural exegesis to help us see the work of the Spirit in unexpected places—such as in the work for justice.

On March 23, 2018, Helen Blier and her teenage daughter attended the March for Our Lives rally in Washington, DC. Unlike many other rallies she had attended in the past, Helen was struck by the "artfully, mindfully crafted practice" designed by the students of Marjory Stoneman Douglas High School "that had nobody over the age of nineteen on the stage, that interspersed critiques . . . of their white privilege" while also "leveraging it as white victims of a shooting over and against the youth of color in places like New York and Chicago and LA who had been fighting gun violence for decades." In between speeches by Parkland youth and youth of color, the program featured performances by Miley Cyrus and Ariana Grande that functioned as "the hymnody of what these kids had grown up with," drawing them all together as a congregation. Then Emma Gonzalez took the stage. Leading the masses in a "liturgy of the saints," Emma named each victim and described what they would never be able to do because they will not grow up, speaking in a rhythmic and repetitive cadence that was all too familiar to Helen, a lifelong Catholic.[24]

And then the silence. Standing still and staring straight ahead, Emma led eight hundred thousand people in a silent meditation and prayer of lament. Helen summarizes the experience as follows: "These kids intuitively knew the rhythm of liturgy. They knew liturgy had sacred texts, it had witness. It had call and response, it had intercessory prayer and Invocation of the Saints. It had hymnody, anamnesis, and then commissioning and sending forth. . . . Was it church? Sure felt like it."[25] Can cultural liturgies train our hearts to love God's kin(g)dom? A liturgy of protest that draws our minds, hearts, and bodies into practices that bring a diverse group of people together in solidarity to cry out for a better world and to show—not just say—what that world can look like in that moment might just be able to do this. Considering this with youth and asking them to look for other places in the world where this kind of vision of the good life is offered can help us make connections between the training in God's *shalom* we receive within the church and the training we sometimes find in the midst of struggles for justice and peace. It can also equip youth to create their own counterformative liturgies to practice out in the world as they seek to overcome silence and transform violence.

Liturgical Exegesis: Reading Our Own Worship Practices

Regardless of your church's denominational affiliation (or lack thereof), its worship services have rhythms and rituals that the congregants come to expect—just try to make changes and see what the reaction is! In addition, most youth groups have their own times and places for gatherings, some designated as worship, some designated as Sunday school or confirmation class, and others simply seen as "hanging out" or fellowship—in addition to special times such as retreats and mission trips. Paying close attention to the "way we do things" can yield insights into how those practices might be forming your hearts.

Consider the weekly worship service:

- Do youth worship separately from the "adults" in the congregation?
- What roles do youth play in worship?
- What practices make them feel welcome in the worship space?
- How does the worshipping community extend welcome to visitors?
- What and how is singing practiced?
- What are the songs or hymns sung most often?

What theological ideas do the lyrics communicate?
How do the tunes make people feel?
Do youth participate in a choir or praise band?
Do they help with Communion, ushering, technology, or special music?
How does that impact their experience of worship?
Does the service include a moment to confess sins and experience an assurance of God's grace?
What kinds of sins are confessed—personal sins only or also societal sins such as poverty, racism, and violence?
What does the congregation commit to in baptism when it bears witness to someone joining the body of Christ?
What is said and done during Communion?
Does your tradition practice an "open table," and what does it mean if it does or does not?
For what and for whom are prayers said aloud?
Are current events avoided or made the focus of preaching and prayer? Which ones, and how?
How are gratitude and sharing of gifts practiced?
How are you sent out into the world at the end?

Look for the places where the church is being shaped to love neighbor, to reconcile with enemies, to imitate role models in the faith, to confess sins of violence and oppression, to speak uncomfortable truths, to receive blessings to go out into the world to bear witness to peace and work for justice—and to do all this alongside youth.

Consider turning a liturgical lens on your regular youth fellowship gatherings. What do people do when they first show up? How are visitors welcomed? What does the youth room look like? How is the furniture arranged? How do you break bread (or eat pizza) together? Do you have opening or closing rituals? Do you have regular practices around cell phone use? How do you engage Scripture or theological concepts? How do you pray? How do you play? Do you sing or make music together? Look for places where you practice hospitality with all participants; where you practice discernment and growing in faith as members make decisions about dating, friendships, education, careers, and everyday moral dilemmas; where you speak the truth in love; where you find Sabbath rest from the stresses of school and extracurriculars; where a young prophet can share an insightful critique of the present or a vision of hope for the future. After reflecting on some of this yourself, consider inviting a small group of youth leaders, or the entire group, to engage in this "liturgical audit" together. You might identify practices you want to keep, modify, or discard.[26]

Reclaiming the Wisdom of Our Churches for a New Era

You also might discover practices you want to add. Smith urges Christians to dig deep in our traditions as resources for shaping our desire for the kin(g)dom. What traditions were once part of the practice of your local church that might be worth reclaiming? Are there archives or elders in the community who can jog the congregational memory of important rituals in past times that built inclusive community, encouraged healing reconciliation, or inspired courageous action? Pull out the old hymnals. What songs once inspired congregations to trust God in the midst of violence and uncertainty, to care for those outside their immediate circle, to bear witness to the radical love of God for a broken world? What treasures lie hidden in plain sight within the worship resources of various denominations?

As an example, in my own denomination, the United Methodist Church (UMC), I can find several treasures within the UMC Book of Worship. We have a tradition of the love feast, something our founder, John Wesley, adapted from the Moravian church. In the early days of Methodism, when ordained clergy were in short supply and traveled long distances from church to church, the Sacrament of the Lord's Supper could not occur often. Laypeople thus adopted the love feast, a group practice of sharing water, bread, and an expression of God's grace (a blessing, word of thanks, or prayer) from one person to the next around a circle.[27] I also find in this book a liturgy for a blessing of the animals service, a tradition that honors God's creation and the peace-building work of Saint Francis of Assisi and invites participants to share with each other the important relationships they have with animals in their lives.[28] These practices build community and can be led by youth themselves, as no ordination or special credentials are necessary.

At YTI, we have adapted the passing of the peace, a practice originally derived from the early Christian ritual of sharing a "holy kiss" during the Eucharist, as a peace-building practice. The holy kiss, or "kiss of peace," once symbolized the passing of the Holy Spirit from one person to another, mingling souls and healing divisions, in line with Christ's teaching that we must reconcile with each other before bringing our gifts to the altar (Matt 5:23–34).[29] While at one time this action really was a kiss (indeed, a kiss on the lips!), churches have long since modified this into a handshake or hug, typically with an expression such as "May the peace of Christ be with you." Often, however, churches substitute a standard time of greeting at the beginning of the service instead of this specific ritual of peace making in preparation for receiving communion—or have eliminated it altogether, recognizing the awkwardness many people feel when pressed to make physical contact with strangers around them.

On the first night of worship at YTI, we anticipate that awkwardness and introduce the practice with an invitation: "At YTI, we practice a ritual known as the passing of the peace. You are invited to greet each other by saying, 'May the peace of Christ be with you.' A traditional response is then, 'And also with you.' These words are accompanied by some sign of reconciliation, which may include a handshake, a high five, a peace sign, or a hug. I invite you to ask each other which signs you prefer to use." We practice this at the *end* of the service because it frees us from setting a time limit or trying to call people back together to continue the service. On the first night or two, community members may greet only a few people and find it awkward to ask consent before offering a physical sign of reconciliation, but it does not take long before the passing of the peace becomes a joyous celebration of friendship in which each member greets every other member, and the group often moves into singing around the piano. And because living in a diverse community inevitably involves conflict at some point, these moments really have become opportunities for members to engage in reconciliation, lament, and care, even as the dancing and singing might be swirling around them. Alumni often remark on how much they miss this ritual in other congregations, noting the awkwardness of exchanging handshakes and pleasantries with strangers who never really become neighbors—even when they sit near each other week after week. What would happen if a church took the passing of the peace seriously? What would happen if your youth group did?

Developing Creative Practices for Overcoming Silence and Transforming Violence Between Sundays

How can fasting, the practice in the wilderness that prepared Jesus for his ministry, and prayer, the practice in the garden that prepared Jesus for his journey toward the cross, be adapted to become regular habits for youth and their leaders who seek to become peace builders and justice seekers? Can we spiritually prepare ourselves through fasting and prayer in ways that might make us less likely to default to violence, denial, or retreat in the face of injustice?

The season of Lent, the forty days of fasting and penitence beginning on Ash Wednesday and ending on Holy Saturday before Easter, intentionally connects to the fasting of Jesus in the wilderness. The different Christian traditions—Orthodox, Catholic, and Protestant; "High Church" and "Low Church"; denominational and nondenominational—observe the weeks leading up to Easter in a wide variety of ways. Some traditions have specific guidelines for full or partial fasts on certain days, others encourage individuals to choose something to "give up" for the season (often sweets, or perhaps cursing), while others may not use the language of "Lent" at all but might at times decide as a congregation to observe a "Daniel fast," abstaining from a long list of foods in replication of the diet the prophet Daniel observed while in exile in Babylon (Dan 1:8–21). Regardless of the specifics, the practice of fasting has deep roots in all religious traditions and is something Christians can adopt and adapt to train our hearts to love rightly.

Fasting reveals many insights: our dependence on our bodies and on the Creator who made our bodies, the privilege of choosing deprivation rather than living in forced deprivation as the result of oppression, how easily we become attached to or distracted by things of lesser importance than love of God and neighbor. While traditional practices of abstaining fully or partially from certain foods and drinks certainly continue to yield such insights, other forms of "wise abstention" can yield new insights and create new habits specific to issues of violence and injustice. For example, I have engaged in Lenten fasts with young people in which we each chose a specific action to give up that would reduce our role in unreflective participation in structural violence or oppression. In preparation for this, each of us had to discern the specific ways we are caught up in systems of power and domination that cause harm to animals, humans, or the earth. Out of this discernment, we each decided on a particular activity to abstain from for the season and declared that intention to the rest of the group. We then agreed to check in weekly on how our fasts were going, offering support and accountability as we engaged in this journey together. Fasts were wide ranging, highly specific to each person's own habits. Some examples include giving up fast food or meat; refusing to purchase items with plastic packaging; logging out of social media accounts that encouraged gossip, bullying, or judgment of others; giving up television, video games, or online videos that focused on violence; disengaging from toxic relationships; refraining from road rage; refraining from arguing with a family member. Such abstentions yielded important insights about how frequently and unthinkingly we often slip into actions or words that demean others, how alluring gossip and self-righteous judgment is, how difficult it is to buy products that are not connected in some way to environmental and human rights violations. We expect to fail frequently: the point is not to "win" the fast but to understand how deeply embedded we all are in habits and cultures that cause harm and to find more life-giving habits to help us resist them.[30]

Christians have always engaged in prayer, but prayer practices that serve to increase one's capacity to engage in prophetic action with love at its root connect particularly with the way Jesus prayed in the garden of Gethsemane. With my students, we have explored a range of prayer practices aimed at training our hearts for peace building and justice seeking, drawing on long tradition as well as creating innovations for our current context. We have walked the streets of our neighborhoods, praying for its inhabitants. We have engaged in guided meditation, in which we sit quietly and imagine individuals, groups, nations, and the planet enveloped in the warm light of God's love.[31] We have taken up the news headlines of the day and prayed in detail for each story of brokenness. We have written prayers on special paper embedded with seeds and then buried them in the soil to allow our prayers to nourish the earth and flourish as flowers to praise God. We have memorized the prayer of Saint Francis, a prayer for enemies such as one found in the *Book of Common Prayer*,[32] the Jesus Prayer, and even the Serenity Prayer to pray daily or even hourly to internalize habits of praying for peace.

Andrew Dreitcer lists several prayer practices drawn from the Christian tradition for learning the way of peace. Some of these include (1) prayer of recollection, in which one sets aside a time and place to meditate on Scripture, listen to meditative music, relax muscles and focus on breathing, or engage in chanting or singing and then invites God's gracious presence into this time; (2) prayer of desire, in which one engages Mark 10:46–51a and responds to Jesus's question, "What do you want me to do for you?" as a way to discover one's deepest desires and longing for God's *shalom* as manifest in that moment; (3) prayer of attentiveness, in which one engages in examination of one's day and notices the details of the people, events, and circumstances around one, considering where one is receiving or giving a sense of peace; (4) prayer with creation, in which one goes out into God's creation and focuses on the presence of God in particular embodiments of God's handiwork; (5) centering prayer, in which one sits for five to twenty minutes in silence, counting one's breath or focusing on a sacred word or phrase in order to quiet one's mind and open up to the presence of God; and (6) prayer in the heat of the moment, in which one learns to pray for one's enemies even in the midst of a conflict.[33] As individuals or as a community, we have many ways to train our hearts in the ways of peace so that when we engage in justice work, or find ourselves in conflict, we can be better prepared to respond in love rather than out of fear or hatred.

You Are What You Love: Becoming the Hands and Feet of Jesus

The gift of Luke's account of the Jesus story is the image of a Godman who prepares for his divine work through processes humans can emulate. From birth to death, Jesus's life follows a pattern of worship, prayer, and fasting that not only shows us that he is the Son of God but shows us how to grow into our own identities as God's children. Jesus engages in worship and spiritual practices to prepare himself to meet the challenges of alluring rival kingdoms and to confront violence and injustice with love and nonviolence. This is the spiritual preparation that made it possible for Bree Newsome to climb the flagpole. This is the kind of worship that brings thousands of people together to lament the senseless loss of young lives and demand change. This is the spiritual preparation that can help our youth become the hands and feet of Christ in the world, working for peace and speaking out for justice in ways that honor the image of God in all. This is the kind of worship and prayer that spills out into the streets.

To the liturgy of the streets we now turn.

Chapter Seven
ACTING IN THE WORLD NONVIOLENTLY

On a hot and humid morning in July 2015, nine scholars and three staff members from the Youth Theological Initiative (YTI) stood on the steps of the Georgia State Capitol carrying signs they had made. Each sign displayed the message the sign holder felt was most important to communicate to the world:

"#BlackLivesMatter"
"When a woman is incarcerated she is expected to give up her freedom, not her soul."
"Justice even for the Voiceless"
"Honk for Justice!"
"Mass Incarceration is not the answer. We need change. #No Second-Class Citizenship"
"No One is Free When Others Are Oppressed"
"Mass Incarceration: Learn the Facts"
"Ban the Box: Give Them a Second Chance"

One sign simply had the words "Mass Incarceration" with a black X marked through it. Another said "This is what theology looks like!! #BlackLivesMatter #ericgarner #icantbreathe #mikebrown #handsupdontshoot."

The scholars and staff could choose how to engage in this demonstration. Some were sitting against a fence, chatting, propping the sign up on their legs. Others stood along the sidewalk, holding their signs at angles for occupants of cars to see and cheering when drivers honked in support. Others chanted loudly—"Black

Lives Matter! Black Lives Matter! Black Lives Matter!"—their signs pulsing to the rhythm of their words. The demonstration was short, about an hour, and small, just the dozen YTI participants, but it made an impact on the people walking to and from the seat of power in Georgia, on the people hanging around in front of the church across the street, and on the young people themselves.

A young Black man who had been walking down the opposite side of the street noticed the group on the capitol steps. In particular, he noticed Michael, a white high school student whose sign read "#BlackLivesMatter." Intrigued by the demonstration, and especially by the sight of a white teenager holding this sign, the man crossed the street and approached Michael, asking him what the group was doing. He had just read Michelle Alexander's *The New Jim Crow* and wanted to know if Michael had read it. Michael had, because it was part of the group's preparation for this moment. Michael, an otherwise quiet student, came alive in this exchange, in which he and the man discussed the book and how it inspired them to act for change. Michael's teacher, Christy Oxendine, snapped a picture of the moment and posted it to Facebook with this caption:

> This exchange and photo is one that really touched my heart today. . . . As I was preparing for today I began thinking, we live in a country where citizens need to stand on the street to help others realize the importance of a certain population. The fact that we need a movement declaring #BlackLivesMatter breaks my heart. I'm reminded of how important it is to be in conversation with one another. We have young people who are ready and willing to speak truth! After spending three weeks with the scholars of #YTI2015 I am hopeful and I know they are doing and will continue to do great things. These are our leaders, not for tomorrow, but for today![1]

Christy had good reason to feel pride and hope as a teacher and youth pastor witnessing this moment. Through much prayer and preparation, she had created the space for the youth to speak up and put into action what they had learned.

Christy led what at YTI is called a "Faith and Justice Contextual." Several different leaders offer courses focused on particular social justice themes, using both traditional classroom and experiential education activities to engage students in connecting their faith with the world. Faith and justice leaders have offered courses on refugees and immigration, technology and the digital divide, food insecurity, gentrification and affordable housing, climate change and environmental racism, and more. Christy chose mass incarceration as her theme, based on her own commitments, awakened by her work interning as a chaplain at a women's prison, as well as her own experience as a Lumbee tribe member and woman seeking to address discrimination across race, class, and gender. The scholars had a menu of faith and justice courses from which to choose, and this mix of Black and white students, from across the United States and several Christian traditions, chose the topic of mass incarceration for their own varied reasons.

The demonstration at the Georgia Capitol was the culminating activity of the class, a final project giving the students a chance to say, and show, what they had learned. They came to this moment of action after significant preparation. During the first week, they read selections from *The New Jim Crow*, watched a clip of one of Alexander's lectures, and visited the Georgia Justice Project, a nonprofit that provides criminal defense for impoverished clients. There they spoke to lawyers engaged in pro bono legal work and to organizers spearheading the "Second Chance for Georgia Campaign"—an effort to reform Georgia state law to expand expungement of criminal records for those returning citizens who have served their time and followed the law for several years after their incarceration.[2] In week two, they read and discussed an essay by Christian ethicist Elizabeth Bounds, "For Prisoners and Our Communities," and watched a TED talk by Bryan Stevenson, founder and executive director of the Equal Justice Initiative. They then spoke with a panel of people, some formerly incarcerated, some working in prisons as chaplains, to consider how Christian ethics and theology relate to the issue of mass incarceration. In week three, they visited the Georgia chapter of 9to5, an organization dedicated to advocating for issues affecting working women, and learned about its role in the Georgia "Ban the Box" campaign, a movement to remove the box printed on employment applications in which formerly incarcerated people are instructed to reveal their criminal history, often resulting in discrimination against applicants who have served their time and are now seeking stable work.[3]

On the final day of their class, Christy offered the students poster board and markers and invited them to make their own signs. What had they learned these past few weeks? What conversation or reading or image had affected their thinking the most? What do they feel the world needs to understand better about this issue? What could they distill into a sign readable by someone driving or walking past them? Each sign expressed a piece of what they had learned and projected it out into the world.[4]

One sign pulled all those pieces together: "This is what theology looks like!!" This is also what peace-building youth ministry looks like.

JESUS MARCHES ON JERUSALEM AND OCCUPIES THE TEMPLE

While all four gospels include the story of Jesus's procession into Jerusalem and cleansing of the temple, we will turn to Mark's account, as he is likely the source for both Matthew and Luke, and his direct and action-packed gospel captures the energy crackling around Jesus as he built his nonviolent revolution.[5]

In Mark 11, Jesus and his disciples engage in an extraordinary campaign of nonviolent action aimed at undermining the religious, political, and economic stranglehold oppressing the Palestinian Jewish people and proclaiming the liberation of God's kin(g)dom. Arriving just outside of Jerusalem, Jesus and his followers stop at the Mount of Olives to set up their basecamp and stage the action. Jesus issues the first order: procure a colt from the nearby village.

Sitting on this colt, Jesus then rides into town with throngs of people laying down branches and clothing to make a royal path for him, all chanting, *"Hosanna!"* (meaning, "Save us!" or "Praise to the Savior!"), blessing him as "the one who comes in the name of the Lord," and proclaiming the "coming kingdom of our ancestor David!" (Mark 11:9–10). Arriving in Jerusalem, Jesus heads straight for the temple, where he does some reconnaissance, and then returns to basecamp for the night with the Twelve (v. 11).

Enacting phase two of the plan, Jesus returns to the city for a nonviolent invasion of the temple. He throws out those who are buying and selling, focusing his action specifically on pushing over the tables used for currency exchange and the chairs of those who sold doves (Mark 11:15). Having captured everyone's attention, Jesus then gives them the justification for his action, quoting the prophets Isaiah and Jeremiah: "Hasn't it been written, *My house will be called a house of prayer for all nations?* But you've turned it into *a hideout for crooks*." The chief priests and legal experts see immediately that Jesus is dangerous but refrain from doing anything at that moment because they can see that the people support him (vv. 17–18). Jesus returns to basecamp but goes to the temple repeatedly thereafter, engaging in a "nonviolent siege"[6] by walking around teaching people and arguing with the legal authorities. He even occupies the spot across from the collection box for the temple treasury, from which he can call attention to the actions taking place (12:41–44).

The march on Jerusalem and occupation of the temple are strategic nonviolent actions designed to speak directly to both the masses of people and the powers that be. As any good nonviolent campaigner knows, understanding your context and designing actions that resonate with the people are crucial for success. Jesus knows his context and is a master of optics. The political context is a nation under occupation by Rome (in Judea, under Pontius Pilate) and by Rome's client kings (in Galilee, under Herod Antipas). The economic context is widespread debt and poverty among the masses, with a small minority (yes, the 1 percent!) controlling not only vast amounts of land but also the banking systems that keep people in debt. The rulers overtaxed the people for their pet building projects and tributes to Caesar, forcing taxpayers to take out loans. Those who fell behind on these debts had to sell themselves into slavery or forfeit their lands to the loan holders. The religious context is a temple system, controlled by the priests and justified legally by the scribes, that collaborates with the political and economic oppression in the name of religious duty. In addition to the sacrificial requirements under Mosaic law, temple taxes added to the financial strain and contributed to the payment of tribute to Rome, while priests offered daily sacrifices in honor of Caesar in exchange for permission to control the temple economy.

In the midst of this context, Jesus chooses to ride into Jerusalem on a colt, making reference to Zechariah 9:9–10, in which the prophet invites Jerusalem to rejoice at the arrival of her king, who, though riding in "humble . . . on a colt," will nonetheless be "righteous and victorious" in ending war and speaking "peace to the nations." The people proclaim Jesus as king, and their cries of *"Hosanna!"* (Save us!) specifically acknowledge him as the leader who has the power to save them. Jesus focuses on the tables of currency exchange and the chairs of the dove sellers because these are the places most oppressive to the poor—to pilgrims held captive to bad exchange rates and to poor people who must resort to sacrificing doves to meet their religious requirements because they do not have the grain, oil, or animal offerings required of more prosperous people. He quotes Isaiah 56:7 to make explicit God's vision of the temple as the gathering place of the marginalized and Jeremiah 7:11 to recall the prophet's condemnation of temple corruption. When Jesus stands near the collection box, he does so to point out the scandal of forcing poor widows to give what they can't afford while the temple authorities live off her sacrifice. In these actions, we see a crowd of people proclaiming Jesus as their savior king in the line of King David, a king who then exposes the exploitation of the temple system as both economic theft and religious sacrilege. No wonder the priests and legal experts saw Jesus as dangerous!

Yet as savvy as Jesus's march on Jerusalem was, the action is the culmination of a much broader strategy. Terrence J. Rynne frames Jesus's entire ministry and teachings as a strategic nonviolent campaign to win over the people to his alternative vision of liberation in the kin(g)dom of God. Jesus begins by recruiting a vanguard—the disciples—and training them (Mark 1:16–20; 3:13–19). He builds strong grassroots support by traveling throughout Galilee preaching in the synagogues and engaging in healings and exorcisms (1:21–45) and begins to draw crowds from increasingly distant areas (3:7–8; 5:1; 7:32; 8:27). He engages members of the religious power structure in debate in hopes of persuading them to his vision (2:6–11; 16–17; 23–28; 3:1–6; 3:22–30, etc.) and appears to have found common ground with some of the legal experts (12:28–34) even in the midst of much arguing and verbal jujitsu (11:27–33; 13:13–17; 13:18–27; 13:35–40). After identifying a committed core, building a movement, and attempting to negotiate with his opposition, Jesus steps up the pressure for change by launching his Jerusalem campaign.[7]

In addition to appreciating his grassroots organizing strategy and mastery of symbolic action, we can take note of several other aspects of nonviolent action that Jesus models. First, Jesus shows us that anger, channeled constructively in nonviolent action and rooted in a commitment to love even those who oppose you, is a valid and even useful emotion in response to injustice. The temple action is meant to be shocking, and though Christian tradition often downplays Jesus's anger in this scene, it can be liberating to acknowledge that anger in the face of unnecessary suffering and exploitation is not only healthy but *Christian*.[8]

Second, Jesus shows us that nonviolent action must be grounded in a vision that seeks the inclusion and salvation of everyone. Jesus was political, but he was not partisan—his vision of the kin(g)dom of God was open not only to peasants but also to the elite, not only to men but also to women and children, not only to Judeans but also to Samaritans and gentiles.

Third, Jesus shows us that engaging in nonviolent action requires risk, and those who choose to engage in it must first assess this risk and make a conscious decision whether to take on this risk before moving forward. On the way to Jerusalem, Jesus pulls aside the Twelve and tells them exactly what is going to happen before the march even begins: "The Human One will be handed over to the chief priests and the legal experts. They will condemn him to death and hand him over to the Gentiles. They will ridicule him, spit on him, torture him, and kill him. After three days, he will rise up" (Mark 10:32–34). He is prepared for the inevitable response of people in power to the threat his action poses, and he wants his core group of followers to understand this so that they will stay unified as the repression intensifies. Though Jesus has counted the cost and prepared himself, unfortunately his vanguard is still not ready to see it through. Despite knowing this, and knowing the risks before him, Jesus chooses to move forward.

Jesus's Jerusalem campaign makes clear that nonviolent action, rightly understood and enacted, is an expression of Christian discipleship. If our churches and our youth choose to follow Jesus by engaging in nonviolent action in our own contexts, we can draw on the wisdom and courage of many before us who have experimented with nonviolence to help us translate our faith commitments into action in the world.

WISE AS SERPENTS, INNOCENT AS DOVES: STRATEGIC NONVIOLENT ACTION FOR SOCIAL CHANGE

Many years ago, when as a young seminary student I was preparing to attend my denomination's quadrennial conference in order to advocate for changing our church's stance condemning homosexuality, a savvy mentor reminded me of Jesus's advice to the Twelve before he sent them out to the cities to proclaim the good news: "Be wise as serpents and innocent as doves" (Matt 10:16 NRSV). Her advice—drawing on Jesus's own wisdom—was meant to encourage me to learn how to operate effectively in the context into which

I was going but at the same time not to give in to the temptation to use unethical means to reach my desired ends. Her advice was invaluable. It was also the core insight of nonviolent strategy.

In my years of teaching nonviolence to youth and adults, I have come to anticipate the misperceptions many have about nonviolence. Though many have a passing familiarity with Mohandas Gandhi and Martin Luther King Jr., and though most students moving through the US educational system will have studied something about the civil rights movement, the unfortunate term "*non*violence"—a term that evokes nothing more than a void, an absence of violence—misleads some into assuming that nonviolence is passive, cowardly, and unrealistic. Nonviolence, they believe, is for people who aren't capable or willing to fight back for what they want, or for people who are fooling themselves with idealistic visions of wolves lying down with lambs. Others assume it is something limited to extreme situations or extraordinary people. Sure, they think, nonviolence worked for Gandhi and King, but those were unusual times in the past, and they were unusual people willing to pay the ultimate sacrifice. Because our history books have made Gandhi and King into larger-than-life figures, we have lost our connection to them as models we could follow. Their teachings, we tell ourselves, are beautiful. But regular people—particularly regular young people—are not like them, so we are not meant to apply their teachings to our own lives.

This is why I prefer to start with the teachings of Gene Sharp.

Gene Sharp—theorist, researcher, and head of the Albert Einstein Institution—has been called the "Machiavelli of nonviolence" and the "Clausewitz of unarmed revolution."[9] His groundbreaking study of nonviolent strategy and catalog of hundreds of examples throughout history of ingenious efforts to resist oppression and overthrow dictators without resorting to arms, *The Politics of Nonviolent Action*, was published in 1973 and is still in print today. As he continued to observe the ways everyday people used nonviolence, in both world-changing events and in lesser-known cases around the world, he gathered wisdom about how nonviolence works and what it takes for it to work well. This wisdom has been used by young people in Serbia to remove Slobodan Milosevic from power in 2000 and by activists in the Arab Spring in 2011. This wisdom is the wisdom of serpents—practical and realistic. And something that young people have used and can use today.

Sharp begins with definitions. Because he wants to highlight the use of nonviolent methods by a wide array of people across cultures and for different purposes, he sets aside the concept of "nonviolence" as defined by religious or ethical beliefs in order to focus on the techniques themselves. He thus uses the terms *nonviolent action* and *nonviolent struggle*. This also underscores the fact that nonviolent action *is* action, not a passive acquiescence to injustice. Nonviolent action is thus also confrontational and is not about avoiding conflict. In fact, it often exacerbates conflict in order to expose the injustice and push people to make changes. While it does require a willingness to engage in confrontation, this is not the same as engaging in violence. And because of this, nonviolent action is accessible to a much broader group of people: without the need to obtain expensive weaponry, skilled training in their use, or physical strength to engage in combat, nonviolent action is available to senior citizens,[10] disabled people,[11] poor people,[12] and of course, young people.[13]

To know how nonviolent action works, however, one must first understand how power works. Sharp defines political power as "the total authority, influence, pressure and coercion which may be applied to achieve or prevent the implementation of the power-holder."[14] On this, advocates of violence and nonviolence agree: you have power if you can make people do what you want them to do. The difference, however, between people who assume that violence is the only or most effective way to make change and those who engage in nonviolent action is in how they understand power. The "monolithic view of power" assumes a top-down model of power: people are dependent on the goodwill of their leaders, coming from a few people at the top who keep power concentrated within their elite circle and pass it on within this small circle. If political power is a monolithic block that has been and always will be, it is easy to conclude that the only way to get rid of those in power is to blow up that block. This is what we see often in history as a *coup d'état*, and it typically results in no real change in the system but rather just a change in the faces at the top.

In contrast to this, Sharp offers the "dependency" or "social view" of power, which flips this dynamic. The rulers at the top, whether politicians, CEOs, school principals, or the president of the student council, are in fact dependent on the goodwill, decisions, and support of the people. Such power is fragile because to make it work, it relies on a continuous flow of support from below, from a wide range of people and institutions. In this view, political power can shift at the moment enough sources of a leader's power are cut off. Sharp lists six sources of political power: (1) authority or legitimacy (the right voluntarily given by the people to the ruler to be considered a legitimate leader), (2) human resources (the number of persons who obey and cooperate or provide special assistance to the leaders), (3) skills and knowledge (the quality of skills, knowledge, and abilities of those people and institutions that supply the leaders' needs), (4) intangible factors (the psychological and ideological habits or attitudes of the people that influence how much people are willing to follow or submit to a leader), (5) material resources (the degree to which leaders can control and use economic systems, property, communication systems, natural resources, etc. to advance their goals), and (6) sanctions (the types of punishments or inducements the leaders can use to force people to obey or punish them for not obeying). These six sources of power are required to establish or retain power and control, but how strong and available those sources are to a leader are in constant flux and utterly dependent on other human beings' willingness to comply in order to supply those sources. Power is dependent on people—this is why "people power" threatens leaders and institutions.

We typically do not realize just how fragile power is, because for the most part, people willingly comply with the wishes of their leaders. Sharp lists the many reasons for this: (1) habit, (2) fear of sanctions, (3) moral obligation, (4) self-interest, (5) a psychological affinity with the leader, (6) indifference, and (7) absence of self-confidence to disobey. Sometimes we obey a rule because it aligns with our own sense of right and wrong: the vast majority of people don't murder not just out of fear of getting caught but also out of a belief that murder is wrong. Sometimes we obey because we simply don't care enough to fight it: some might dislike limiting one's liquids to three-ounce bottles to go through an airport security checkpoint but don't consider it a good use of time to resist that rule, until eventually compliance with that rule becomes a habit. And sometimes we obey because we trust the leader and believe certain leaders have our best interests at heart: citizens who maintained their social distancing and hygiene practices during the COVID-19 pandemic because they trusted the advice of epidemiologists and doctors.

Here's an illustration of how this works: take the power of school administrators to make students follow a dress code. If school administrators want the students to dress a particular way, the students and faculty must be willing to comply for it to work. Administrators depend on students and faculty recognizing the administrators' authority to create school policy. They depend on teachers to stand in the hallways and enforce the code by telling people to tuck in their shirts or by sending them to the principal's office for violating the code. They depend on teachers, parents, and students to understand the dress code and the administrators' legal rights to enforce the code. They depend on the vast majority of students to be in the habit of doing what adults tell them to do. They depend on their ability to control students' access to the school, to use space for detention or in-school suspension, to take up and lock away inappropriate clothing, and to reward students with "nonuniform days" or other incentives to comply. And finally, they depend on sanctions of detention, demerits, suspension, public humiliation, or informing parents to scare students into following the code. Most students follow a dress code without much resistance, however, because they're in the habit of following school rules, because they do indeed fear the sanctions, because it is in their self-interest to comply in order to get rewards, because they really just don't care, because they don't believe they could mount a successful resistance to it, because they trust their school administrators to know what is best for them, or because they honestly believe a dress code helps improve their learning environment. But if—*if*—enough students thought a particular dress code was wrong, whether because it was simply too constricting of their freedom of expression or because it perpetuated sexist double standards or racist assumptions about "respectability," they could fight it.

How they might fight it comes down to understanding the various methods of nonviolent action. Having collected hundreds of historical examples over years of research, Sharp categorized the methods of nonviolent action into three classes and distilled them into a list of 198 methods, with an analysis of their appropriateness for different contexts. The first class of nonviolent action includes "actions to send a message," or protest and persuasion.[15] This class includes many of the actions with which Americans are most familiar: speeches, petitions, carrying signs, wearing buttons, vigils, marches, processions, teach-ins, moments of silence, and walkouts. Christy and her students demonstrating at the Georgia Capitol falls into this category. So does Jesus's march on Jerusalem.

The second class of nonviolent action includes "actions to suspend cooperation and assistance," or noncooperation with social, economic, or political institutions or practices. This class includes boycotts, strikes, refusal to pay taxes or debts, civil disobedience—any action in which people refuse to engage or dramatically slow down their engagement in something in order to bring it to a halt. Church denominations that have supported consumer boycotts or refused to invest their funds in companies engaged in immoral activities or human rights violations fall into this category. So do Rosa Parks's refusal to abide by the segregation code on a Montgomery bus and the yearlong boycott this sparked. So does Jesus's refusal to comply with Sabbath laws in order to heal and exorcise demons.

The third class of nonviolent action includes "methods of disruption" or "nonviolent intervention." Rather than withdrawing from something (as in noncooperation), these actions jump into a situation in an effort to make change. This class includes sit-ins, obstruction (e.g., chaining oneself to a tree or building), creating alternative transportation or communication systems, deliberately seeking to be arrested in order to fill the jails, and occupation of a space. The Greensboro lunch counter sit-ins fall into this category. So does the Occupy Wall Street movement. So does Jesus's occupation of the temple.

For any of these actions to work, however, nonviolent campaigners must take seriously the importance of preparation, commitment, and strategy, says Sharp. It is this emphasis on careful planning, risk assessment, and training that has earned Sharp the comparison to military strategists like Clausewitz. While the tools may be nonviolent, nonviolent action is still a conflict, and to win a conflict, you must be smarter and more committed than your opponent. Before launching nonviolent action, Sharp advises the nonviolent struggle group to conduct a "strategic estimate," or "a calculation and comparison of the strengths and weaknesses of the nonviolent struggle group and of that group's opponents." This involves gathering information about the general conflict situation, the issues at stake, the objectives of the nonviolent group as well as those of the opponent group, the resources and dynamics of the opponent group itself, the resources and dynamics of the nonviolent group, the role of third parties and their allegiances to either side of the conflict, and the current degree of dependency on the six sources of power that each group has.[16] Using this information, the nonviolent struggle group draws up a strategic plan that includes an overall vision for what they want to accomplish, a specific set of demands, a time line of different phases of action they plan to follow, the specific methods they want to use, and a plan for what to do if they fail, succeed, or meet with partial success. They must also assess the degree to which their members are willing to endure repression once the campaign is launched. We see Jesus engaging in strategy in his recruitment and teaching of the disciples; his promotion of their training as they go out to the cities to evangelize and then return to assess and regroup; his building of popular support for his vision through preaching, teaching, healings, and exorcisms; and his use of various methods of persuasion, protest, noncooperation, and intervention.

Sharp primarily envisions an audience of people suffering under dictators or discriminatory institutions, in which failure to engage in nonviolent action without a careful strategy might very well result in significant costs in lives and livelihoods. But his understanding of how nonviolent action works and what it takes to make it work well serves as a resource for smaller-scale actions and reminds us that nonviolent action is not successful merely because we sincerely believe our cause is just. Even Jesus encouraged us to be wise as serpents.

Elijah Shoaf, a youth delegate to our United Methodist Church (UMC) Annual Conference meeting, knew the importance of planning and strategy. In 2019, when he was seventeen years old and a junior in high school, he drafted a resolution calling on our annual conference to provide education and resources to support the mental health of LGBTQIA+ youth, particularly those at risk for suicide. Knowing that resolutions relating to support of LGBTQIA+ persons had been voted down in the past by a decision-making body still dominated by theologically conservative power brokers, Elijah set out to draft an "unsinkable" resolution that avoided the mistakes of the past. He researched how to write strong resolutions and focused his wording on "doing good" by helping vulnerable youth rather than making a political statement because, as Elijah explained, "people want to do good, but they also want you to respect their opinions. I think the biggest mistake the UMC is making right now is connecting the current divide in the church with the current divide in this country. Because the stigma caused by that connection is making sure that nothing gets done."[17] Leading up to the conference, he sought advice and feedback. At the conference, he enlisted a strategic list of people to speak in favor of the resolution, paying attention to the optics of age, race, gender, and sexual orientation. On hearing about his efforts, others came forward to offer their support, including two whose powerful testimonies directly addressed the questions and counterarguments of the opposition and appealed to the consciences and goodwill of everyone in the room.

In what was originally expected to be a close vote, 80 percent of the conference delegates voted in favor of the resolution, after defeating by a similar margin an attempt to water down the resolution by striking down the language focused on LGBTQIA+ youth. For the first time in its history, this particular UMC Annual Conference passed with overwhelming support a resolution that expressed love for and offered meaningful resources to a segment of the population so recently harmed by the decisions of its denomination.

Elijah was wise as a serpent in his strategy and innocent as a dove in his grounding of that strategy in his faith in human goodwill and love of neighbor.

LEARNING TO BE BOTH WISE AND INNOCENT: PEDAGOGICAL PRACTICES FOR NONVIOLENT ACTION

In the previous chapters, activities common to youth ministry—fellowship, Sunday school, Bible study, mission trips, worship, and prayer—became opportunities for growing in faith while also growing as peace builders and justice seekers. But these skills may not translate into action in the world (in communities, schools, families, churches) unless they are connected with the preparation and strategies that wise people—Mohandas Gandhi, Martin Luther King Jr., Rosa Parks, Bree Newsome, and high school student Elijah Shoaf—and Jesus Christ himself understood and modeled. At YTI, we have experimented with learning activities that have helped our young people discern not only where God might be calling them to address the world's deep hunger but also how to claim their power to do this. It is in discovering that they are leaders *now*, not merely leaders of the future, who can make a difference in the contexts in which they live that we believe deep gladness can be found.[18] It is also how they can resist the formative power of the images of incomplete adult and precocious delinquent. Preparing and supporting young people as they overcome silence and transform violence must become explicit components within the youth ministry curriculum. The activities described here contribute to this work.

Teaching Concepts of Nonviolence

I have had the opportunity to teach Sharp's basic theory of nonviolence with young people in high school assemblies, classrooms, and small groups. Sharp worked hard to make his ideas accessible to everyday people, and they can be grasped easily by young people once you connect them with illustrations from their own contexts, as in the dress code example above.[19] As a way to explain the social or dependency theory of power, I have used two illustrations in particular. One is a clip from the film *A Bug's Life* in which the main antagonist, Hopper, explains to the other grasshoppers why the one ant who stood up to him is a threat: "You let one ant stand up to us then they *all* might stand up. Those puny little ants outnumber us a hundred to one, and if they ever figure that out, there goes our way of life. It's not about food. It's about keeping those ants in line."[20] Hopper knows that his power is dependent on the other grasshoppers staying unified and vigilant doing his bidding and on the ants remaining afraid of them and ignorant of the power in their numbers.

Another illustration is an activity using the game Jenga. I stack up the Jenga blocks as you would for a typical Jenga game on a freestanding table where all the students can see. I then tell the students that each block represents a person in the room. The Jenga tower stands as long as every single block remains in its designated place. I then pull one block out and name someone in the room, explaining that this person has decided no longer to participate in holding up this particular tower. I take that block and set it aside.

I then take out another block and name another person, explaining that this person supports the first person and wants to join them in this new vision of a different way of living, and set aside that block with the other one. Using my best Jenga skills, I try to pull out as many blocks as I can *without* causing the tower to fall over so that I can name many people in the room and heighten the excitement. The students become enthralled waiting for the tower to fall, and they often beg to be named so that they can be the one whose defection causes the tower to collapse. Once it falls, the blocks scatter everywhere, and the idea of the fragility of political power becomes clear.

As a way to explain the different methods of nonviolent action, I have employed several resources. One is to play the "nonviolent method game." This requires having a copy of volume two of Sharp's original trilogy *The Politics of Nonviolent Action: The Methods of Nonviolent Action* (1973), which lists the 198 different methods of nonviolent action along with examples from history. I read out the different methods[21] and ask students to stop when they hear one that intrigues them, then look it up in the book and read the description. Students are usually curious to hear about numbers 22 (protest disrobings), 30 (rude gestures), 35 (humorous skits and pranks), and 178 (guerilla theater) and can easily relate to actions such as number 133 (reluctant and slow compliance—how long have they waited to take out the trash or clean their room?) or 136 (disguised disobedience—how creatively have they found ways to use their phones when they were told not to?). I sometimes ask them to pick a number between 1 and 198 and use that to find entries to read to them. The stories Sharp has collected are intriguing and sometimes funny (e.g., he describes a protest in which a group of people ate beans before going to a meeting in an enclosed space and gassed out the meeting!) and enlivens their imaginations about the creativity and long history of nonviolent action—most of which they have never learned about in school. Add to this an invitation to brainstorm examples they *have* learned about in school or elsewhere and encourage them to pay attention to the news to find examples taking place currently. I keep a file of examples, particularly of young people, so that I can introduce students to the stories of everyday people engaging in nonviolent action for a wide range of causes, including those they care about most.[22]

One can also use the list of 198 actions to try to identify the nonviolent actions that biblical characters have taken: are the Hebrew midwives in Exodus 1:15–22 engaging in number 134 (nonobedience in absence of direct supervision) or 136 (disguised disobedience)? What are Shadrach, Meshach, and Abednego doing—number 63 (social disobedience), 120 (refusal of public support), 141 (civil disobedience of "illegitimate laws"), or 195 (seeking imprisonment)? Are the disciples in Acts 2:42–47 engaging in number 192 (alternative economic institutions) or 174 (establishing new social patterns)? What is Zacchaeus doing—number 104 (professional strike) or 113 (strike by resignation)? How many different nonviolent actions can we find Jesus doing? Is Jesus actually suggesting that people should *not* pay taxes to Caesar in Matthew 22:15–22?[23] How often does he disobey the Sabbath laws? The purity laws? Is the Sermon on the Mount a "teach-in"?[24] Such conversations help uncover the revolutionary actions of people of faith and further expand students' awareness of the tools of nonviolent action available to them.

Sharp aims to create a wide umbrella under which people of all kinds of religious, philosophical, and pragmatic perspectives can engage in nonviolent action—even if they are not pacifists and even if they might believe violence is justified in other contexts. While Sharp's theory makes nonviolence more imaginable for more people, we Christians are called to root our nonviolence in Jesus's teachings and actions. We must then go beyond Sharp's concepts to teach Christian nonviolence principles as well. Central to Christian nonviolence is Jesus's call to love our enemies and pray for those who harass us so that we can "be complete" in showing love to everyone, just as God does toward us (Matt 5:43–48).[25] It is this commitment to love our opponents even as we struggle with them that characterizes the work of Gandhi and King and still guides the nonviolent action of many people, Christians and non-Christians alike. This commitment to enemy love, however difficult it may be to achieve, is not an impossible ideal and in fact is quite practical. In *The Nonviolence Handbook: A Guide for Practical Action*, Michael Nagler reminds us that "right intentions" are just as important as "right means." When engaging in a nonviolent action, Nagler advises us to stop thinking of a dispute "as a zero-sum game where, in order for me to win, you have to lose." Rather, when faced with an issue of injustice or violence that we want to fight, we should remember, "It is not me against you but you and me against the problem; there is a way for both of us to grow": by turning "an argument into a problem-solving session, a dispute into a learning experience, and eventually a feeling of alienation into an awareness of unity."[26] Keeping the focus on the overall goal, and resisting the temptation to become bitter toward one's opponent in defeat or to humiliate one's opponent in victory, can in fact yield greater, more sustainable victories in the long run. As Elijah Shoaf knew, he could accomplish his goal more effectively by assuming his opponents' desire to "do good," and once he accomplished his goal, he did not frame it as a defeat of "evil" people who do not know compassion but expressed gratitude for the compassion the conference was showing a vulnerable population. The Nashville lunch counter protestors did not flaunt their victory but agreed to refrain from using their new freedoms to patronize lunch counters for a time in order to de-escalate the tensions and allow store owners to save face. Gandhi wanted the British not just to leave but to leave as friends.[27] Jesus appeared to Saul to convert him, not to strike him dead, turning a persecutor of his followers into his most zealous disciple. When teaching nonviolence with youth, we must keep the principle of love in the forefront.

Teaching Theological Reflection on Social Issues

As wise nonviolent actors know, oppressive systems maintain their power in part by hiding the full extent of their harm. One benefit of participating in mission and service trips as described in chapter 5 comes from stepping outside of our particular location within "the Game of Life" in order to see how the system works, revealing the violence and exploitation embedded in a system that some are not meant to see as more than just their personal lot in life while others are not meant to see at all. Once the concept of structural oppression becomes clearer, students can begin to see how it operates all around them—and how it connects to their faith. One activity we use is inspired by the quotation attributed to theologian Karl Barth that one must do theology with "the Bible in one hand, and the newspaper in the other."[28] I bring in a variety of print newspapers and spread them out on a table. I invite students to break up into pairs or small groups and look through the newspapers to identify a headline, photo, or ad that points to suffering or harm experienced by a group or individual that they feel is unreasonable or unjust. Using a worksheet to guide them through a series of questions, the group tries to learn as much as they can about the situation depicted in the article or image and can use their phones to do further research if they desire. The group then brainstorms images or stories from the Bible in which a group or individual experiences unnecessary or unjust suffering or harm. To aid in this, I have available multiple Bibles, concordances, and Bible dictionaries and encourage students to use biblegateway.com or other online resources. Rather than trying to find a story that directly matches up to the situation in the newspaper—difficult if not impossible to do in most cases—the students should be looking for Bible stories that help them think about suffering and harm more generally from a faith perspective: What can these stories teach us about what God wants for God's creation? What can they show us about how God wants *us* to respond to situations of injustice or suffering? Returning to the newspaper article or image, the students can then look at it through the lens of Scripture. Given what the Bible suggests to us about what God wants for God's creation, and what God wants us to do in situations of injustice, how should we as Christians understand what is happening in this news article? What might we be called to do?

Toward the very end of our time together at YTI, we invite the scholars to create "kairos documents." The Greek term *kairos* means "opportune or appointed time of God," a special moment, different from everyday time (*chronos*), in which people of faith are called to repentance, conversion, and action.[29] Drawing on the history of Christian public witness ranging from the Barmen Declaration resisting the Nazi takeover of the German church, the South African kairos document resisting apartheid, and the many subsequent kairos documents written by Christian groups calling for action to respond to injustice in their contexts around the world—in Central America, Kenya, Zimbabwe, India, Palestine, and the United States[30]—we invite scholars to identify an issue of injustice or violence about which they are particularly passionate, group the scholars together based on their common interests, and guide them through a process of writing a brief document calling on people of faith to act in particular ways to address the injustice or violence they identify. Their kairos documents have three components: (1) *social analysis* (i.e., a summary description of the issue, including what it is, who is involved [those harmed by the situation, those benefitting from it, those perpetuating it], and their interpretation of why it is taking place), (2) *theological reflection* (i.e., biblical principles or concepts from their Christian tradition[s] that speak to the issue), and (3) *call to action* (i.e., specific, doable actions that they want Christians or people of conscience to do that they believe can make a difference in this issue). By working in groups, students can help each other brainstorm ideas and distill their thoughts into direct, short sentences to fit on poster board or butcher paper and adults can rove from group to group to help them refine their work further. In addition to Bible resources and internet access available for their research, we also have plenty of different colored markers available so that scholars can decorate their kairos documents and sign their names to them at the end. Groups then present their documents to each other, and we discuss which actions they see as doable for themselves and their peers, as well as their churches or schools.

Preparation for Action: Self-Reflection and Strategic Planning

In his study of Gandhi as a political strategist, Gene Sharp notes that one of Gandhi's crucial insights was a recognition of the importance of changing the attitudes of the people in order to help them change their patterns of obedience to and cooperation with structures that oppress them. It is one thing to talk in general terms about the fragility of power and its dependence on the cooperation of everyday people; it is quite another to convince specific people that in order for them to make meaningful progress on their own social justice goals, they must change their own ways of passive acceptance of the status quo.[31] A field of study called "peace psychology" can help with this.

In his essay "Building Confidence for Social Action," Barry Childers develops a list of social actions people typically use to advance the cause of peace. His list of 101 actions includes activities such as joining an organization, writing a letter to the editor of a local paper, circulating a petition, calling congressional representatives, attending or leading an educational event, running for public office, volunteering for an organization, distributing leaflets on a street corner, hosting a debate, boycotting a company, giving money to an organization, and many others. Childers suggests we use this list for several purposes: to "(a) assess your unique interests and skills in relation to social action, (b) evaluate the difficulties that particular kinds of activities present so that you can better understand them, and (c) choose the most appropriate tasks and build confidence in undertaking them."[32] While the list can be used alone in personal reflection, Childers recommends that individuals gather in a support group to discuss their responses and identify ways they can help each other build confidence and courage to try new activities. Next to each item is a blank line, where people using the list can indicate how difficult it would be for them to do that particular action (very hard [VH], moderately hard [MH], or fairly easy [FE]). As readers go through the list, they should give their gut-level reaction in marking the level of difficulty. After completing the list, readers can go back to the items marked VH and reflect on why those are so difficult for them. Finally, readers can review the list to identify one item marked MH that appeals to them and that represents something they could do now, perhaps with the help of others. Individuals can discuss in pairs or in the group their answers to this, as well as identify a plan for moving forward with the chosen MH activity they'd like to try.

I have taken Childers's list and adapted it for the context of Christian youth. To connect with the context of faith, I have added activities such as prayer, speaking to your youth group or Sunday school class, preaching a sermon, writing a resolution for your denominational decision-making body, developing a mission activity for the church, and supporting a faith-based organization working for justice. To connect with the context of young people, I have added activities such as starting or joining a school club, advocating for change in school policy, connecting an issue to a school project, and using social media to raise awareness. In using this inventory with different groups of young people, I have been struck by how few actions they have considered doing and how much encouragement they need to realize how much they can do now, as young people, without waiting until they are "old enough" to make a difference.

I have also connected the concept of gift inventories to the work of social justice. As youth are discerning particular issues about which they are most passionate, I ask them to reflect on the following: What gifts or skills do I have to contribute toward addressing this issue? (Please consider a full range of gifts, skills, and resources, because you might be able to contribute in some creative and surprising ways. For example, do you like to do research? Do you like to write? Draw? Dance? Preach? Are you good at leading meetings? Are you good at getting people to resolve conflicts? Are you good at organizing events? Are you comfortable talking to new people? Are you good at doing "behind-the-scenes" work like stuffing envelopes, packing and sorting, making signs, etc.?) I offer examples of skills and gifts that they already employ in their hobbies, in their friendship circles, at church and school, pointing out how much of what they already love to do or are good at doing can be directed toward creative work for change.

Gene Sharp intended his research for very practical purposes: he wanted to increase the success of those groups who desired to win their rights and freedom using nonviolent means. He thus offered detailed advice to activists on how to prepare and plan their campaigns. Although his advice assumes larger groups of people with bigger targets for action—workers fighting for better working conditions, marginalized groups fighting for civil rights, citizens fighting for democracy—it can be scaled down and adapted for more modest contexts and goals. Taking the example of the dress code above, students who found their school's policy to be sexist or racist, or simply too constrictive of their self-expression, could develop a strategic approach to changing it. This would involve conducting research into past attempts at changing dress code policies in other schools as well as any social science research into the impact of dress (and by implication, dress codes)—positive and negative—on learning. It would involve surveying other students and the faculty to find out how much support there would be for changing the policy. It would involve identifying parents, faculty, and administrators who might be allies, as well as those who might oppose the campaign. It would involve learning the process for making changes in school policies. It would involve a plan for negotiating with those charged with drafting policies and perhaps offering a solution up front—for example, establishing a task force with students as well as faculty and administrators to rewrite the policy. And it would involve a plan for what to do if negotiations fail, including decisions about what sorts of nonviolent actions students and allies would take and when: Will they use social media to gain attention to their cause? Will they organize everyone to disobey the dress code on a particular day? Will they stage a walkout? Leaders in the movement would need to discern how far they would be willing to take the campaign and what sanctions they are willing to endure—Detention? Suspension? Expulsion? Pressure from their peers? Pressure from their parents? As an adult walking alongside such youth, you can review with them the questions Sharp encourages nonviolent campaigners to consider, helping them see the importance of thinking through beforehand what they want to do, how they want to do it, how much support they have to do it, and how much they are willing to work to do it.

These and many other activities can help young people learn the concepts of nonviolent action and prepare themselves mentally and logistically to overcome the disempowering images of youth as incomplete adults and precocious delinquents and embrace the image of God within them. These and many other activities can help "young, scrappy, and hungry" leaders, like Starr Carter in *The Hate U Give* and Alexander Hamilton, live into their vocation as God's peace builders and justice seekers.

THIS IS WHAT THEOLOGY LOOKS LIKE: GOING OUT TOGETHER AS SHEEP AMONG WOLVES

As passionately as Christy Oxendine felt about mass incarceration, she worked with her students as a skillful teacher and caring youth pastor, not as a charismatic revolutionary leading children into danger. She intentionally framed the activity on the Georgia Capitol steps as a "demonstration," avoiding the term *protest*, because she knew from her own experience that *protest* was a weighted term that often made people nervous, evoking images of dangerous crowds or angry exchanges—something she was confident would not be the case on their day of action. She invited the students to participate at the level at which they felt comfortable and to choose for themselves what messages to write on their signs. They had chosen her class for a reason, and after nearly three weeks of studying the issue, all of them wanted to make their voices heard. Her hope was to introduce the students to the possibility of nonviolent action through direct experience, and she provided a low-risk way to do that. Teaching nonviolence to youth, though admittedly edgy, does not—and should not—needlessly put young people in harm's way. But given the amount of violence and oppression already taking place in the lives of young people, we would be irresponsible not to concede that they are *already* in harm's way.

Of course, as young people begin to claim their power as agents of change, their actions may very well involve risk—from demerits to suspension to arrest and yes, perhaps to physical harm done by those who oppose them. Emma Gonzalez and David Hogg of the March for Our Lives movement and Isra Hirsi and Greta Thunberg of the Climate Strike movement, as well as many others, regularly receive hate mail and death threats. Bree Newsome risked arrest and tasing by police in order to take down the South Carolina flag. Jonathan Butler risked death by engaging in a hunger strike. But they also received support and mentoring by adults and peers who were willing to walk alongside them as they discerned the most effective ways to reach their goals of justice and freedom, assessing the risk responsibly, and weighing those risks against their commitments to their cause and to their family, friends, and futures.

The youth with whom we work may not be seeking to overthrow dictators or lead global movements, but they are yearning to free themselves from white supremacy, ephebiphobia, gender norms that control and objectify their bodies, educational policies that destroy their self-esteem and love of learning, ecclesial practices that discount them as full members of the body of Christ, and economic policies that destroy their environment and saddle them with debt. Once young people learn about the forces of injustice and violence that affect them, and once they begin to understand that they have the power and voice to do something about this, they want to act. And to do so is not ancillary to their faith; it is their deepest expression of it. Our job as supportive adults who want their freedom and want to discover our own freedom alongside them, our job as followers of Christ, is to help them do this well: as strategically as serpents, as nonviolently as doves.

CONCLUSION

IMAGES THAT SHAPE OUR WORK

At the conclusion of *The Hate U Give*, after her speech, after the riot, after her family begins cleaning up the burned-out remains of her father's store, Starr proclaims her commitment to continue to fight for justice. She has been on a journey. Many people accompanied Starr on this journey: her father helped her come to understand structural oppression and the history of racism in the United States; her mother reassured her that bravery is not fearlessness but acting for justice in spite of one's fears; her lawyer-activist mentor, Ms. Ofrah, coached her in public speaking, set up a media interview, and handed her the megaphone; her Williamson friends Maya (Asian American) and Chris (white), wrestling with their own identities in relation to Starr's, helped her recognize the nuances of race and class and the complexities of allyship; and her Garden Heights friend Kenya held her accountable to her own stated values, pushing her to greater self-honesty. And Black Jesus, with arms outstretched over Garden Heights, oversaw it all. With one foot in the middle-class, white community of Williamson High and one foot in the underserved Black community of Garden Heights, Starr found a way to overcome the domestication of one world in order to resist the criminalization of the other.

Though "the world called him thug," Starr calls the boy whom police had murdered at point-blank range by his name, Khalil, and insists the world see him as "a hazel-eyed boy with dimples" who deserved a longer, better life. And though she is propelled into her activism by her personal relationship with one particular boy, she now sees that she has become part of a movement that goes beyond the story of one boy destroyed by the harmful image of the precocious delinquent. She is part of the Movement for Black Lives, and she names some of the communion of saints who propel her to keep working for change: Oscar. Aiyana. Trayvon. Rekia. Michael. Eric. Tamir. John. Ezell. Sandra. Freddie. Alton. Philando. And Emmett Till. Starr is also propelled in her work knowing that others are also fighting for justice, "realizing and shouting and marching and demanding." She makes a promise to Khalil never to forget. She makes a promise to herself never to be quiet.[1]

I write this in the summer of 2020. To Starr's list, we must add Ahmaud Arbery, Breonna Taylor, and George Floyd, and many others who are being brutalized as I write. Across the world, people young and old are using their voices, and their bodies, to defend Black lives—and at great risk. Now more than ever, youth workers have a chance to walk, or march, alongside young people, helping them discern how best to connect their faith to nonviolent action for meaningful change.

Starr makes a promise. I have made my own promise, a promise not to forget the "young, scrappy, and hungry" people who took great risks to overcome silence and transform violence:

> John Laurens, friend of Alexander Hamilton, son of a wealthy slave owner, who worked tirelessly to
> establish a plan for enslaved Africans to gain their freedom through serving as soldiers to fight in the
> Revolutionary War
>
> Hans Scholl, Sophie Scholl, Christoph Probst, Alexander Schmorell, and Willi Graf, University of Munich students who formed a secret group, the White Rose, to speak out against the Nazis through graffiti and pamphlets, encouraging readers to engage in nonviolent resistance and sabotage the war effort
>
> Minnijean Brown, Elizabeth Eckford, Ernest Green, Thelma Mothershed, Melba Patillo, Gloria Ray, Terrence Roberts,

Jefferson Thomas, and Carlotta Walls, the "Little Rock Nine," who integrated Little Rock Central High School in 1957

Ezell Blair Jr., David Richmond, Franklin McCain, and Joseph McNeil, the "Greensboro Four," college students influenced by Gandhi's nonviolent protest techniques whose carefully organized lunch counter sit-in at the Woolworth's in downtown Greensboro, North Carolina, sparked a sit-in movement that spread to fifty-five cities in thirteen states in 1960

The more than one thousand students, some as young as six years old, who marched in downtown Birmingham, Alabama, in 1963, braving water hoses, police clubs, biting dogs, and jail cells to protest segregation

Mary Beth Tinker, the thirteen-year-old junior high school student from Des Moines, Iowa, whose insistence on wearing a black armband to school to protest the Vietnam War led to the 1969 landmark *Tinker v. Des Moines* Supreme Court ruling in favor of students' rights to free speech in public schools

Srdja Popovic and the members of Otpor! (Resistance!), the Serbian student group that successfully organized a mass, nonviolent movement to remove dictator Slobodan Milosevic from power in 2000, creatively adapting the strategies of Gene Sharp using humor, music, and electoral politics

Jasilyn Charger, Joseph White Eyes, and Trenton Casillas-Bakeberg, three Lakota Sioux youth who formed the One Mind Youth Movement in 2015, at first to address the wave of suicides among their peers and then to mount a campaign against the Keystone XL pipeline, whose route threatens the water source for their people

Autumn Peltier, member of the Wikwemikong First Nation in northern Ontario, who fights for universal clean drinking water for Indigenous peoples

Emma Gonzalez, David Hogg, Sam Zeif, Julia Cordover, Cameron Kasky, Jaclyn Corin, Kyle Kashuv, Ariana Klein, Alfonso Calderon, and Lorenzo Prado, the Marjory Stoneman Douglas High School students who launched the #NeverAgain movement and the March for Our Lives in 2018 in response to the shooting of seventeen of their classmates on February 14, 2018, in Parkland, Florida

J. J. Warren, Elijah Shoaf, and the 2019 confirmation class of First United Methodist Church, Omaha, all United Methodist Church young people who have used their voices to proclaim a gospel message of compassion toward and inclusion of LGBTQIA+ persons in our denomination

Greta Thunberg, who began her campaign to fight climate change by skipping school to engage in a solitary strike in August 2018, inspiring a global movement, and Isra Hirsi, cofounder of the US Youth Climate Strike in 2019, whose group organized millions of students across 120 countries to walk out of their classes and demand climate action, shaming their elders for their complacency

Patrisse Khan-Cullors, Alicia Garza, and Opal Tometi, who cofounded Black Lives Matter in response to the 2013 acquittal of George Zimmerman after his murder of Trayvon Martin, a hashtag that became a global movement to fight anti-Black racism, inspiring young people on the streets across the United States

Rachel Corrie, my cousin, who at age eleven delivered a public speech articulating her dream to end global hunger and at age twenty-three, in 2003, went to Gaza, Palestine to engage in nonviolent action to protect the lives and livelihoods of Palestinian civilians

The members of the Conclave, youth and youth workers who fact-checked me, read drafts of chapters, and cheered me on to the finish line

Each of these young people holds me accountable to my own work, as a teacher, a scholar, an activist, a youth minister, and a Christian, and reminds me that young people should never be underestimated.

This book represents my hope that youth ministry can do more than entertain or contain; it can equip and liberate. That it can convince adults and youth themselves that young people are more than the image of incomplete adults or precocious delinquents; that they are the *imago Dei*. That our ministries follow a Christ who saved us through the way he lived, not just through the way he died. This book represents my hope that adults and young people can bridge the generation gap, overcoming the silence and transforming the violence this gap has perpetuated. This book represents my hope that youth ministry, as in all Christian living, will focus on peace building and justice seeking, bringing God's *shalom* ever nearer as we live in expectant hope of full consummation.

NOTES

CHAPTER ONE

1. Lin-Manuel Miranda, "Alexander Hamilton," MP3 audio, track 1 on *Hamilton: An American Musical (Original Broadway Cast Recording)*, Atlantic Records, 2015; Lin-Manuel Miranda, "My Shot," MP3 audio, track 3 on *Hamilton*. Lyrics can be found online at *Hamilton: An American Musical (Original Broadway Cast Recording)*, Genius, accessed January 21, 2021, tinyurl.com/4564vz2g.
2. Theologian Johann Baptist Metz uses the concept of "dangerous memory" to describe subversive memories of the victims of history that are threatening to the status quo. They remind us that current reality, institutions, and societies could be other than they are. Johann Baptist Metz, *Faith in History and Society: Toward a Practical Fundamental Theology* (New York: Seabury, 1980).
3. Todd Andrilk, "Ages of Revolution: How Old Were They on July 4, 1776?," *Journal of the American Revolution*, August 8, 2013, https://tinyurl.com/hc7eelu.
4. Richard Linklater, dir., *Dazed and Confused* (1993; Universal City, CA: Gramercy Pictures, 1998), DVD.
5. Angie Thomas, *The Hate U Give* (London: Walker, 2017), 35.
6. Thomas, 284, 331, 334, 444.
7. Thomas, 287.
8. Thomas, 30, 88, 31, 334.
9. David White, *Practicing Discernment with Youth: A Transformative Youth Ministry Approach* (Cleveland: Pilgrim, 2005).
10. These two terms were inspired by reading Wesley Ellis, "Human Beings and Human Becomings: Departing from the Developmental Model of Youth Ministry," *Journal of Youth and Theology* 14, no. 2 (2015): 119–37; and Anthony M. Platt, *The Child Savers: The Invention of Delinquency*, expanded 40th anniversary ed. (New Brunswick, NJ: Rutgers University Press, 2009).
11. Juliet Schor, *Born to Buy: The Commercialized Child and the New Consumer Culture* (New York: Scribner, 2004).

12 Joseph F. Kett, *Rites of Passage: Adolescence in America 1790 to the Present* (New York: Basic Books, 1977); Nancy Lesko, *Act Your Age! A Cultural Construction of Adolescence* (New York: Routledge Falmer, 2001); Robert Epstein, *Teen 2.0: Saving Our Children and Families from the Torment of Adolescence* (Fresno, CA: Quill Driver, 2010).
13 Kett, *Rites of Passage*, 217.
14 Paula S. Fass, *The End of American Childhood: A History of Parenting from Life on the Frontier to the Managed Child* (Princeton, NJ: Princeton University Press, 2016), 135.
15 Thomas Hine, *The Rise and Fall of the American Teenager: A New History of the American Adolescent Experience* (New York: HarperCollins, 1999), 255.
16 Fass, *End of American Childhood*, 163–70.
17 Epstein, *Teen 2.0*.
18 Lesko, *Act Your Age!*, 27–35.
19 Hine, *Rise and Fall of the American Teenager*, 111.
20 Kett, *Rites of Passage*, 89.
21 Fass, *End of American Childhood*, 58–61.
22 Jon Savage, *Teenage: The Creation of Youth Culture* (New York: Penguin, 2007), 65.
23 Epstein, *Teen 2.0*, 61; see also Sheila O'Connor, "When 'Incorrigible' Teen Girls Were Jailed," *New York Times*, November 14, 2019, https://nyti.ms/2qSCegu.
24 Platt, *Child Savers*.
25 John DiIulio, "The Coming of the Super-Predators," *Weekly Standard*, November 27, 1995, https://tinyurl.com/y3g9p5zc.
26 Robin Templeton, "Superscapegoating: Teen 'Superpredators' Hype Set Stage for Draconian Legislation," FAIR, January 1, 1998, tinyurl.com/hlos3mgd.
27 Kirk A. Astroth, "Are Youth at Risk?," *Journal of Extension* 31, no. 3 (1992), https://archives.joe.org/joe/1993fall/a6.php.
28 The term *kingdom* used for the advent of the reign of God through the return of Jesus Christ comes out of the political context of empire in the Bible. Jesus's use of the word flips this political meaning on its head. Some Christians today prefer to leave out the g and speak of it as a *kin-dom*, an egalitarian vision of all of God's children gathered together as siblings in Christ. I will use *kin(g)dom* to hold both usages together.

CHAPTER TWO

1. This narrative has been adapted from one written by former Youth Theological Initiative (YTI) assistant director Rachelle Green, who granted permission to include it here.
2. Names matter. Instead of calling our youth "high school students" or "teens" or "kids," we call them "scholars" to confirm their capabilities as young people and treat them with respect.
3. Name has been changed.
4. Nonviolent communication is a technique for communication in moments of conflict. It can go far to de-escalate tensions and address issues. Marshall Rosenberg, *Nonviolent Communication: A Language of Life* (Encinitas, CA: PuddleDancer, 2003).
5. Holy listening is a practice of paying close attention to each other as we share our stories. Dori Baker and Joyce Mercer discovered the importance of holy listening for young people while interviewing them for their research. Interviewees noted that no adult had ever asked them such meaningful questions and paid such close attention to their answers and that this experience of receiving unhurried, engaged attention was healing and liberating. See Baker and Mercer, *Lives to Offer* (Cleveland: Pilgrim, 2007).
6. Peter Block, *Community: The Structure of Belonging* (San Francisco: Berrett-Koehler, 2008), 5.
7. Block, 37, 40.
8. Block, 47.
9. Block, 48.
10. Block, xii.
11. *YTI Manual* (unpublished manual, 2016), 5.
12. Block, *Community*, 32.
13. Nathan Stucky has explored the role of Sabbath in youth ministry in *Wrestling with Rest: Inviting Youth to Discover the Gift of Sabbath* (Grand Rapids, MI: Eerdmans, 2019).
14. For a discussion of the way YTI staff have built trust with young people through play rather than surveillance, see Elizabeth W. Corrie, "Crossing Over: Transforming the War on Kids through Ministries with Youth," in *Conflict Transformation and Religion: Essays on Faith, Power, and Relationship*, ed. Ellen Ott Marshall (New York: Palgrave Macmillan, 2016), 81–96.
15. Block, *Community*, 114.
16. Block, 179.
17. For mutual invitation, see Eric Law, *The Wolf Shall Dwell with the Lamb: A Spirituality for Leadership in a Multicultural Community* (St. Louis: Chalice, 1993), 79–88. For circle processes, see Kay

Pranis, *The Little Book of Circle Processes: A New/Old Approach to Peacemaking* (Intercourse, PA: Good Books, 2005).
18. Lorraine Stutzman Amstutz and Judy H. Mullet, *The Little Book of Restorative Discipline for Schools: Teaching Responsibility, Creating Caring Climates* (Intercourse, PA: Good Books, 2005).
19. See note 4 in this chapter.

CHAPTER THREE

1. Yonat Shimron, "Protesting Methodist LGBTQ Policy, Confirmation Class Takes a Pass," *Religion News Service*, April 29, 2019, https://tinyurl.com/y27oaq4f.
2. Shimron.
3. Thanks to the Reverend Kent Little of First United Methodist Church, Omaha, for details of this story.
4. Shimron, "Protesting Methodist LGBTQ."
5. Mary Jane Pearce Norton, *Credo: Confirmation Guide for Parents, Mentors, and Adult Leaders* (Nashville: Abingdon, 2015).
6. Shimron.
7. The remainder of this chapter comes from Elizabeth W. Corrie, "Deliberative Democratic Theological Education: A Proposal for Youth Ministry That Builds Peace," *Religious Education* 115, no. 2 (2020), https://doi.org/10.1080/00344087.2020.1768471. Reprinted with permission.
8. We will explore the central role of the temple for Jesus in chapters 6 and 7.
9. Howard W. Stone and James O. Duke, *How to Think Theologically*, 3rd ed. (Minneapolis: Augsburg Fortress, 2013), 1–2, 20–21, 25.
10. Stone and Duke, 15.
11. Stone and Duke, 20–21.
12. Stone and Duke, 4.
13. Stone and Duke, xiv.
14. Wisconsin Institute for Public Policy and Service, "The Three D's: Discussion, Debate, and Deliberation," cited in Stacie Molnar-Main, *Deliberation in the Classroom: Fostering Critical Thinking, Community, and Citizenship in Schools* (Ashland, OH: Kettering Foundation, 2017), 61. This source is also available to users with access to ProQuest through Emory University here: https://tinyurl.com/y5n4tbhb.
15. Wisconsin Institute for Public Policy and Service, 61.
16. Wisconsin Institute for Public Policy and Service, 62–63.
17. The deliberative democracy movement comes out of concerns about the decline of civic engagement in the United States since the

mid-twentieth century. See Theda Skocpol, *Diminished Democracy: From Membership to Management in American Civil Life* (Norman: University of Oklahoma Press, 2003); and Peter Levine, *We Are the Ones We Have Been Waiting For: The Promise of Civic Renewal in America* (New York: Oxford University Press, 2013).

18 Molnar-Main, *Deliberation in the Classroom*, 14.
19 Molnar-Main, 17.
20 Molnar-Main, 20.
21 Molnar-Main, 13.
22 The National Issues Forums website has resources for hosting deliberative forums, in the community and in the classroom: "Home," National Issues Forums, accessed September 12, 2019, https://www.nifi.org/en/home.
23 Molnar-Main, *Deliberation in the Classroom*, 45.
24 Brad Rourke, *Developing Materials for Deliberative Forums* (Dayton, OH: Kettering Foundation, 2014), available at https://tinyurl.com/y37xa4bl.
25 Rourke, 11.
26 Rourke, 11.
27 I added Scripture in order to address some of the biblical illiteracy common among Christian youth, as noted in Christian Smith and Melissa Lundquist Denton, *Soul Searching: The Religious and Spiritual Lives of American Teenagers* (New York: Oxford University Press, 2005), 131–37.
28 Patricia A. Wilson, "Deep Democracy: The Inner Practice of Civic Engagement," *Fieldnotes: A Newsletter of the Shambala Institute*, no. 3 (February 2004).

CHAPTER FOUR

1 Timothy Beal, *The Rise and Fall of the Bible: The Unexpected History of an Accidental Book* (New York: Houghton Mifflin Harcourt, 2011), 116–17.
2 Beal, 9.
3 Beal, 27.
4 Beal, 21.
5 Beal, 175, 179, 196.
6 Leticia A. Guardiola-Sáenz and Frank M. Yamada, "Culture and Identity," in *The Peoples' Companion to the Bible*, ed. Curtiss Paul DeYoung et al. (Minneapolis: Fortress, 2010), 9.
7 Choi Hee An, "Women, Culture, and the Bible," in DeYoung et al., *Peoples' Companion to the Bible*, 73–74.

8   Johanna W. H. van Wijk-Bos, "Responsible Christian Exegesis of Hebrew Scripture," in DeYoung et al., *Peoples' Companion to the Bible*, 79.

9   Fernando Segovia, "Toward a Hermeneutics of the Diaspora: A Hermeneutics of Otherness and Engagement," in *Reading from This Place*, vol. 1, ed. Fernando F. Segovia and Mary Ann Tolbert (Minneapolis: Fortress, 1995), 57–73, 59, 70–71.

10 For Lauren's own reflections on her method, as well as more in-depth descriptions of her recommended best practices, see Lauren Calvin Cooke, "Any Questions?," laurencalvincooke.wordpress.com, November 8, 2018, https://tinyurl.com/y22dsomt; and Lauren Calvin Cooke, "Turning Questions into Conversation," laurencalvincooke.wordpress.com, June 5, 2019, https://tinyurl.com/y4zmaocu.

11 See Michael Prior, *The Bible and Colonialism: A Moral Critique* (Sheffield, UK: Sheffield Academic Press, 1997); Rosemary Radford Reuther, *Sexism and God-Talk: Toward a Feminist Theology* (Boston: Beacon, 1983); and Amy-Jill Levine, *The Misunderstood Jew: The Church and the Scandal of the Jewish Jesus* (San Francisco: HarperCollins, 2006).

12 See Norman K. Gottwald, "Framing Biblical Interpretation at New York Theological Seminary: A Student Self-Inventory on Biblical Hermeneutics," in *Reading from This Place*, 251–61. The version we draw on for the Youth Theological Initiative (YTI) is "A Self-Inventory for Bible Readers," found in DeYoung et al., *Peoples' Companion to the Bible*, xxix–xxxii.

13 Orit Kent, "Interactive Text Study: A Case of *Hevruta* Learning," *Journal of Jewish Education* 72, no. 3 (2006): 206.

14 Orit Kent, "A Theory of *Havruta* Learning," *Journal of Jewish Education* 76, no. 3 (2010): 219.

15 Kent, 220.

16 Rebecca Shargel, "*Havruta* Goes to the University: *Havruta*-Style Text Study in a College Education Class," *Journal of Jewish Education* 85, no. 1 (2019): 8.

17 Elie Holzer and Orit Kent, *A Philosophy of Havruta: Understanding and Teaching the Art of Text Study in Pairs* (Brighton, MA: Academic Studies Press, 2013).

18 Holzer and Kent use a questionnaire in the beginning of their sessions to help individual students consider the gifts and challenges they bring to a *havruta* pair, and they use the responses to determine how to match people. See Holzer and Kent, "Setting the Stage for Havruta Learning," chap. 3 in *Philosophy of Havruta*, 60–89; and Holzer and Kent, appendix 3 in *Philosophy of Havruta*, 219–21.

CHAPTER FIVE

1 Portions of this narrative come from an article originally published with Duke Divinity School's Faith and Leadership online learning resource. See Elizabeth Corrie, "Empowering Youth for Change by Connecting Theology and Social Analysis," Faith and Leadership, March 7, 2017, https://tinyurl.com/y5vr573a.

2 Iris Marion Young describes structural oppression as "systemic constraints on groups" resulting from "causes . . . embedded in unquestioned norms, habits, and symbols, in the assumptions underlying institutional rules and the collective consequences of following those rules." This "extended sense" of oppression, which goes beyond the image of a few people knowingly dominating another group, "refers to the vast and deep injustices some groups suffer as a consequence of often unconscious assumptions and reactions of well-meaning people in ordinary interactions, media and cultural stereotypes, and structural features of bureaucratic hierarchies and market mechanisms—in short, the normal processes of everyday life." It is this understanding of oppression that we try to replicate in a game that resembles everyday life. See Iris Marion Young, *Justice and the Politics of Difference* (Princeton, NJ: Princeton University Press, 2012), 41.

3 Merriam-Webster defines a microaggression as "a comment or action that subtly and often unconsciously or unintentionally expresses a prejudiced attitude toward a member of a marginalized group." *Merriam-Webster*, s.v. "microaggression (n.)," accessed January 21, 2021, https://tinyurl.com/yd3ut4gg.

4 This simulation game is effective but carries risks, as it can hit close to home for those who experience violence and discrimination as part of their daily lives. Immense care goes into setting it up and assigning roles, monitoring the situation as it takes place, and carefully debriefing afterward, as indicated later in this chapter. Space does not allow for the full description of the curriculum here, but the author welcomes invitations to consult with those who want to try it in their own contexts. It is also focused on preparing for work in US contexts and would have to be drastically changed for overseas mission work or for youth in other contexts.

5 Pui-lan Kwok, *Discovering the Bible in the Non-biblical World* (Maryknoll, NY: Orbis, 1995), 71.

6 Smith and Denton, *Soul Searching*.

7 Barbara Jacoby et al., *Service-Learning in Higher Education: Concepts and Practices* (San Francisco: Jossey-Bass, 1999), 5.

8 See Michael E. Sherr, Diana R. Farland, and Terry A. Wolfer, "The Role of Community Service in the Faith Development of Adolescents," *Journal of Youth Ministry* 6, no. 1 (2007): 43–54; Kraig Beyerlein, Gary Adler, and Jenny Trinitapoli, "The Effect of Religious Short-Term Mission Trips on Youth Civic Engagement," *Journal for the Scientific Study of Religion* 50, no. 1 (2011): 780–95; Jeremy Myers and Mark J. Jackson, "The Freedom of a Teenager: Vocation and Service Learning as the Future of Youth Ministry," *Dialog* 47, no. 4 (2008): 327–38; and Jenny Trinitapoli and Stephen Vaisey, "The Transformative Role of Religious Experience: The Case of Short-Term Missions," *Social Forces* 88, no. 1 (2009).

9 Tania D. Mitchell, David M. Donahue, and Courtney Young-Law, "Service-Learning as a Pedagogy of Whiteness," *Equity and Excellence in Education* 45, no. 4 (2012): 612–29; Joseph A. Erickson and Susan E. O'Connor, "Service-Learning: Does It Promote or Reduce Prejudice?," in *Integrating Service Learning and Multicultural Education in Colleges and Universities*, ed. Carolyn R. O'Grady (Mahwah, NJ: Lawrence Erlbaum, 2000), 59–70; Andrew Root, "The Youth Ministry Mission Trip as Global Tourism: Are We OK with This?," *Dialog* 47, no. 4 (2008): 314–19; Terence D. Linhart, "They Were So Alive! The Spectacle Self and Youth Group Short-Term Mission Trips," *Missiology* 34, no. 4 (2006): 451–62; Eric Hartman, Cody Morris Paris, and Brandon Blache-Cohen, "Fair Trade Learning: Ethical Standards for Community-Engaged International Volunteer Tourism," *Tourism and Hospitality Research* 14, nos. 1–2 (2014): 109.

10 Eric Hartman et al., *Community-Based Global Learning: The Theory and Practice of Ethical Engagement at Home and Abroad* (Sterling, VA: Stylus, 2018), 8. This source is also available to users with access to ProQuest through Emory University here: https://tinyurl.com/y2qonefs. On the problems of international service in orphanages and medical mission trips, see "Videos," Campus Compact, accessed February 23, 2020, https://compact.org/global-sl/video/.

11 Richard Slimbach, "Flights of Peril and Privilege," Campus Compact, October 7, 2019, accessed February 17, 2020, https://tinyurl.com/y6m88tye.

12 Doug Banister, "Rethinking the $3000 Missions Trip," *Christianity Today*, July 23, 2013, accessed February 17, 2020, https://tinyurl.com/y4hkz74z.

13 Hartman et al., *Community-Based Global Learning*. See also "The Community-Based Global Learning Collaborative," Campus

Compact, accessed January 21, 2021, https://compact.org/global-sl/; and Hartman, Paris, and Blache-Cohen, "Fair Trade Learning," 108–16.

14 Hartman, Paris, and Blache-Cohen, "Fair Trade Learning," 114.

15 Tania D. Mitchell, "Traditional vs. Critical Service-Learning: Engaging the Literature to Differentiate Two Models," *Michigan Journal of Community Service Learning* 14, no. 2 (2008): 50–65.

16 I am influenced by Musa Dube's reading. See *Postcolonial Feminist Interpretation of the Bible* (St. Louis: Chalice, 2000).

17 Kimberlé Crenshaw, "Demarginalizing the Intersection of Race and Sex: A Black Feminist Critique of Antidiscrimination Doctrine, Feminist Theory and Antiracist Politics," *University of Chicago Legal Forum* 1989, no. 1, article 8.

18 Mitchell, "Traditional vs. Critical Service-Learning," 59, 61.

19 Sam Marullo and Bob Edwards, "From Charity to Justice: The Potential of University-Community Collaboration for Social Change," *American Behavioral Scientist* 43, no. 5 (2000): 903.

20 Randy Stoecker, *Liberating Service Learning and the Rest of Higher Education Civic Engagement* (Philadelphia: Temple University Press, 2016), 47.

21 Stoecker, 49–51, 58.

22 These dynamics are most famously illustrated in experiments such as Stanley Milgram's study of obedience to authority and Philip Zimbardo's Stanford Prison Experiment. See Zimbardo, *The Lucifer Effect: Understanding How Good People Turn Evil* (New York: Random House, 2008).

23 Walter Wink, *The Powers That Be: Theology for a New Millennium* (New York: Doubleday, 1999), 29–31.

24 Wink, 31.

25 We can begin to take this struggle seriously by following ethical guidelines for our service and mission trips. See Hartman, Paris, and Blache-Cohen, "Fair Trade Learning," 108–16; and "Fair Trade Learning," Campus Compact, accessed February 23, 2020, https://compact.org/fair-trade-learning/. For Holy Land pilgrimages, we can look to ethical tourism guidelines developed by the people in the region. See Palestinian Initiative for Responsible Tourism, "A Code of Conduct for Tourism in the Holy Land: A Palestinian Initiative," Alternative Tourism Group Study Center, accessed January 21, 2020, tinyurl.com/59344p7v.

26 Discussed in Kwok, *Discovering the Bible*, 75.

27 Discussed in Dube, *Postcolonial Feminist Interpretation*, 172–177.

28 David W. Scott, *Crossing Boundaries: Sharing God's Good News through Mission* (Nashville: Wesley's Foundery, 2019), 6–7.

CHAPTER SIX

1. Heba Farrag, "The Role of the Spirit in #BlackLivesMatter Movement," USC Center for Religion and Civic Culture, June 24, 2015, https://tinyurl.com/yywrlrsg.
2. Almeda M. Wright, *The Spiritual Lives of Young African Americans* (Oxford: Oxford University Press, 2017), 160–65.
3. Wright, 159.
4. Louis Lucero II, "What Emma González Said without Words at the March for Our Lives Rally," *New York Times*, March 24, 2018, https://tinyurl.com/yd99t2oy.
5. James Quaeally, "For Ferguson Demonstrators, Thanksgiving Is a Moment of Respite," *Los Angeles Times*, November 27, 2014, https://tinyurl.com/yyp2rpmz.
6. Charlotte Alter, Suyin Haynes, and Justin Worland, "The Conscience," *Time*, December 13, 2019, https://tinyurl.com/yya4xpc4.
7. James K. A. Smith, *Desiring the Kingdom: Worship, Worldview, and Cultural Formation*, Cultural Liturgies, vol. 1 (Grand Rapids, MI: Baker Academic, 2009), 33.
8. Smith, 46.
9. James K. A. Smith, *You Are What You Love: The Spiritual Power of Habit* (Grand Rapids, MI: Brazos, 2016), 10.
10. Smith, 7.
11. Smith, 10–22.
12. Smith, *Desiring the Kingdom*, 83.
13. Smith, 45.
14. Smith, 93–103.
15. Smith, 115–16.
16. Smith, 116–17.
17. Smith, 104–5.
18. In describing these forces as demonic, I am allowing for a range of interpretations regarding the existence and form of "the devil," who appears in the Lukan passage as an individual entity. Whether you believe that the devil is an individual entity that intervenes in the world or that the "demonic" consists in the ethos created by systems of domination that exceeds the sum of the actions and inactions of individual humans, or some other view of how evil operates in the world, the "demonic" here indicates the evil within which we are caught up, knowingly and unknowingly, when we participate in systems that cause harm and oppression to others. For a nuanced view of evil, the demonic, violence, and oppression, see Walter Wink, *Engaging the Powers: Discernment and Resistance in a World of Domination* (Minneapolis: Fortress, 1992).

19 This includes political leaders who use the church doorstep for assertions of power.
20 Smith, *Desiring the Kingdom*, 212; Smith, *You Are What You Love*, 91, 130, 152–53.
21 Smith, *Desiring the Kingdom*, 84.
22 In *Wrestling with Rest*, Nathan Stucky asks a group of high school students to keep a daily time log for a week. After completing this log, they go through and identify which activities they consider restful. This exercise reveals how little Sabbath rest young people have and how even rest becomes stressful, as youth worry about falling behind.
23 Monique W. Morris, *Pushout: The Criminalization of Black Girls in Schools* (New York: New Press, 2016); and Victor M. Rios, *Punished: Policing the Lives of Black and Latino Boys* (New York: New York University Press, 2011). On the impact of school policy on young people, see Cevin Soling, dir., *The War on Kids* (New York: Spectacle Films, 2009), DVD; and John Taylor Gatto, *Dumbing Us Down: The Hidden Curriculum of Compulsory Schooling*, 25th anniversary ed. (Gabriola Island, BC: New Society, 2017).
24 Helen Blier, "Reflections" (PowerPoint presentation, Candler School of Theology, Emory University, April 26, 2019).
25 Blier, "Reflections."
26 A resource for this is Dorothy C. Bass and Don Richter, eds., *Way to Live: Christian Practices for Teens* (Nashville: Upper Room, 2002).
27 "The Love Feast," Discipleship Ministries of the United Methodist Church, November 14, 2014, https://www.umcdiscipleship.org/resources/the-love-feast.
28 Various denominational resources: "A Service for the Blessing of Animals," Discipleship Ministries of the United Methodist Church, accessed April 8, 2020, tinyurl.com/54chxmcc; "Catholic Prayer: Book of Blessings: Order for the Blessing of Animals," Catholic Culture, accessed April 8, 2020, tinyurl.com/4gb2zbzn; and "Seasons of Creation and St. Francis Day Resources," Episcopal Church, accessed April 8, 2020, tinyurl.com/2vhvsfsn. See also Jeff Brumley, "Baptists Embrace Pet Blessings," Baptist News Global, October 22, 2012, https://tinyurl.com/yy24717e.
29 Kathy Black, "The Reconciling Body and the Passing of the Peace," *Liturgy* 24, no. 1 (2008): 26–32.
30 I have also engaged in a fast focused on our engagement in consumerism. See Elizabeth W. Corrie, "Stopping the Zombie Apocalypse: Ascetic Withdrawal as a Tool for Learning Civic Engagement," in *Teaching Civic Engagement*, ed. Forrest Clingerman and Reid Locklin (Oxford: Oxford University Press, 2016), 143–60.

31 I adapted this from a peace meditation developed by Joanna Macy in "Taking Heart: Spiritual Exercises from Social Activists," in *Peace Is the Way: Writings on Nonviolence from the Fellowship of Reconciliation*, ed. Walter Wink (Maryknoll, NY: Orbis, 2000), 135–42.
32 "For Our Enemies," bcponline.org, accessed April 8, 2020, https://www.bcponline.org/Misc/Prayers.html.
33 See Andrew Dreitcer, "Prayer Practices for the Way of Peace," in *Choosing Peace through Daily Practices*, ed. Ellen Ott Marshall (Cleveland: Pilgrim, 2005).

CHAPTER SEVEN

1 Christy Oxendine, "This exchange and photo is one that really touched my heart today," Facebook, July 23, 2015, https://tinyurl.com/yxryjjqs.
2 See Second Chance for Georgia Campaign (website), accessed April 28, 2020, https://www.secondchancegeorgia.org.
3 See 9to5 (website), accessed April 28, 2020, https://9to5.org; "Georgia Chapter," 9to5, accessed April 28, 2020, https://9to5.org/chapter/georgia/; and Ban the Box Campaign (website), accessed April 28, 2020, https://bantheboxcampaign.org.
4 Five years later, Michael explained to me why he chose, as a white person, to make and hold a sign that said "Black Lives Matter": "I felt a magnetic attraction to the slogan because it emphatically contradicted a foundational and apparent but nevertheless unspoken assumption in America that Black lives *don't* matter. I remember reasoning if the arrival of the three-word phrase on the national stage could rapidly draw headlines and visceral opposition, it must contradict deeply held views, and I wanted to square any sub/unconscious sympathy I had for those unspoken cultural assumptions with a conscious affirmation of what I rationally held to be true." In other words, he decided to carry that particular sign in order to confront his own implicit biases and live into a more antioppressive way of being. Michael Robertson, Facebook message to author, May 7, 2020.
5 Since André Trocmé's *Jesus and the Nonviolent Revolution* was first published in English in 1973, numerous scholars in biblical studies, social ethics, and theology have built on the thesis that Jesus's life and teachings, understood within their Palestinian Jewish context, offer a model of Christian nonviolence that is meant to be adapted by Christians to their own lives, even today. My interpretations of Jesus's actions here are informed by this scholarship. See

John Howard Yoder, *The Politics of Jesus: Vicut Agnus Noster*, 2nd ed. (Grand Rapids, MI: Eerdmans, 1994); Richard A. Horsley, *Jesus and the Spiral of Violence: Popular Jewish Resistance in Roman Palestine* (San Francisco: Harper & Row, 1987); Obery M. Hendricks Jr., *The Politics of Jesus: Rediscovering the True Revolutionary Nature of Jesus' Teachings and How They Have Been Corrupted* (New York: Doubleday, 2006); and Terrence J. Rynne, *Jesus Christ Peacemaker: A New Theology of Peace* (Maryknoll, NY: Orbis, 2015).

6 Ched Myers, *"Say to This Mountain": Mark's Story of Discipleship* (Maryknoll, NY: Orbis, 1996), 146.

7 See Rynne, *Jesus Christ Peacemaker*, 45–58.

8 Christian feminist ethicist Beverly Harrison famously lifted up the importance of anger in the face of injustice in "The Power of Anger in the Work of Love: Christian Ethics for Women and Other Strangers," *Union Seminary Quarterly Review* 36, no. 1 (1981): 41–57.

9 Mark Engler, "The Machiavelli of Nonviolence: Gene Sharp and the Battle against Corporate Rule," *Dissent*, Fall 2013, https://tinyurl.com/y5wdqre3. Niccolò Machiavelli was an Italian diplomat and philosopher known for his book *The Prince*, which advises strategic manipulation of power. Carl von Clausewitz (1780–1831) was a Prussian general and military theorist.

10 See the Gray Panthers (website), accessed January 22, 2021, http://www.graypanthersnyc.org; and "Grannies for Peace," Women Against War, accessed January 22, 2021, https://tinyurl.com/y69p3jwq.

11 See ADAPT (website), accessed January 22, 2021, https://adapt.org.

12 See the Poor Peoples' Campaign (website), accessed January 22, 2021, https://www.poorpeoplescampaign.org.

13 See March for Our Lives (website), accessed January 22, 2021, https://marchforourlives.com; and "Mighty Times: The Children's March," Zinn Education Project, accessed January 22, 2021, https://tinyurl.com/y6gmjfrr.

14 Gene Sharp, *The Politics of Nonviolent Action*, Part 1, *Power and Struggle* (Boston: Porter Sargent, 1973), 7–8.

15 Gene Sharp, *Waging Nonviolent Struggle: 20th Century Practice and 21st Century Potential* (Boston: Porter Sargent, 2005), 49–65, 51–54.

16 Sharp, 526, 528.

17 Email communication with Elijah Shoaf, April 23, 2020.

18 Theologian and pastor Frederick Buechner described vocation as "the place where your deep gladness and the world's deep hunger meet." Frederick Buechner, "Vocation," frederickbuechner.com, July 18, 2017, https://tinyurl.com/yyj4l49u.

19 To supplement my summary here, see Sharp, *How Nonviolent Struggle Works* (Boston: Albert Einstein Institution, 2013). Free resources available at Albert Einstein Institution (website), accessed January 22, 2021, https://www.aeinstein.org.
20 John Lasseter and Andrew Stanton, dir., *A Bug's Life* (1998; Emeryville, CA: Pixar Animation Studios, 2003), DVD.
21 The handout that lists the 198 types of methods (without the examples from history) is available here: "198 Methods of Nonviolent Action," Albert Einstein Institution: Advancing Freedom with Nonviolent Action, accessed January 22, 2021, https://tinyurl.com/y2tzqblp.
22 Films can also be useful. For example, Teaching Tolerance offers films and teaching resources for free: "Film Kits," Teaching Tolerance, accessed May 1, 2020, https://tinyurl.com/yy69kqc6.
23 See Horsley, *Jesus and the Spiral of Violence*, 306–17.
24 Significant scholarship on Matthew 5 has suggested that Jesus was teaching creative nonviolent responses to the economic and political oppression his hearers were facing. Walter Wink is best known for this (see *Engaging the Powers*, 175–93). See also William M. Swartley, ed., *The Love of Enemy and Nonretaliation in the New Testament* (Louisville, KY: Westminster John Knox, 1992).
25 For biblical scholarship on the significance of Jesus's teachings on enemy-love, see Wink, *Engaging the Powers*, 263–77; and Yoder, *Politics of Jesus*, 112–33.
26 Michael N. Nagler, *The Nonviolence Handbook: A Guide for Practical Action* (San Francisco: Berrett-Koehler, 2014), 14.
27 This idea becomes clearer in film. The 1982 feature film *Gandhi* remains a compelling way to show students both Gandhi's wise strategy as well as his deep commitment to love of his opponents. The documentary series *A Force More Powerful* also shows these commitments in action. The episode titled "Nashville: We Were Warriors" shows the amount of training the college students underwent and the role of negotiation and compromise Diane Nash and others used to secure their success while deescalating the tensions created by their sit-ins. Clips from this video, as well as teacher resources, can be found at the following: "A Force More Powerful," International Center on Nonviolent Conflict, accessed May 1, 2020, https://tinyurl.com/ybba4cqn.
28 The full lesson plan for this activity may be found at the following: Elizabeth Corrie, "Seeking Joy through Seeking Justice," Yale Youth Ministry Institute, accessed May 4, 2020, https://tinyurl.com/y4y3p8rw.
29 Robert McAfee Brown, *Kairos: Three Prophetic Challenges to the Church* (Grand Rapids, MI: Eerdmans, 2000).

30 For more on the tradition of Kairos documents, see Gerald West, "Tracing the 'Kairos' Trajectory from South Africa (1985) to Palestine (2009): Discerning Continuities and Differences," *Journal of Theology for Southern Africa* 143 (July 2012): 4–22.
31 Sharp, *Waging Nonviolent Struggle*, 37.
32 Barry Childers, "Building Confidence for Social Action," in *Working for Peace: A Handbook of Practical Psychology and Other Tools*, ed. Rachel M. MacNair (Atascadero, CA: Impact, 2006), 9–15.

CONCLUSION

1 Thomas, *Hate U Give*, 442–44.

SELECTED BIBLIOGRAPHY

Amstutz, Lorraine Stutzman, and Judy H. Mullet. *The Little Book of Restorative Discipline for Schools: Teaching Responsibility, Creating Caring Climates.* Intercourse, PA: Good Books, 2005.

Astroth, Kirk A. "Are Youth at Risk?" *Journal of Extension* 31, no. 3 (1993). https://archives.joe.org/joe/1993fall/a6.php.

Baker, Dori Grinenko, and Joyce Ann Mercer. *Lives to Offer.* Cleveland: Pilgrim, 2007.

Bass, Dorothy C., and Don Richter, eds. *Way to Live: Christian Practices for Teens.* Nashville: Upper Room, 2002.

Beal, Timothy. *The Rise and Fall of the Bible: The Unexpected History of an Accidental Book.* New York: Houghton Mifflin Harcourt, 2011.

Beyerlein, Kraig, Gary Adler, and Jenny Trinitapoli. "The Effect of Religious Short-Term Mission Trips on Youth Civic Engagement." *Journal for the Scientific Study of Religion* 50, no. 1 (2011): 780–795.

Block, Peter. *Community: The Structure of Belonging.* San Francisco: Berrett-Koehler, 2008.

Childers, Barry. "Building Confidence for Social Action." In *Working for Peace: A Handbook of Practical Psychology and Other Tools,* edited by Rachel M. MacNair, 9–15. Atascadero, CA: Impact, 2006.

Corrie, Elizabeth W. "Crossing Over: Transforming the War on Kids through Ministries with Youth." In *Conflict Transformation and Religion: Essays on Faith, Power, and Relationship,* edited by Ellen Ott Marshall, 81–96. New York: Palgrave Macmillan, 2016.

———. "Deliberative Democratic Theological Education: A Proposal for Youth Ministry That Builds Peace." *Religious Education* 115, no. 2 (2020): 233–244. https://doi.org/10.1080/00344087.2020.1768471.

———. "Empowering Youth for Change by Connecting Theology and Social Analysis." Faith and Leadership. March 7, 2017. https://tinyurl.com/y5vr573a.

———. "Stopping the Zombie Apocalypse: Ascetic Withdrawal as a Tool for Learning Civic Engagement." In *Teaching Civic Engagement,* edited by Forrest Clingerman and Reid B. Locklin, 143–160. Oxford: Oxford University Press, 2016.

Crenshaw, Kimberlé. "Demarginalizing the Intersection of Race and Sex: A Black Feminist Critique of Antidiscrimination Doctrine, Feminist Theory and Antiracist Politics." *University of Chicago Legal Forum* 1989, no. 1, article 8.

DeYoung, Curtiss Paul, Wilda C. Gafney, Leticia Guardiola-Saenz, George E. Tinker, and Frank Yamada, eds. *The Peoples' Companion to the Bible*. Minneapolis: Fortress, 2010.

DiIulio, John. "The Coming of the Super-Predators." *Weekly Standard*, November 27, 1995. https://tinyurl.com/y3g9p5zc.

Dreitcer, Andrew. "Prayer Practices for the Way of Peace." In *Choosing Peace through Daily Practices*, edited by Ellen Ott Marshall, 36–64. Cleveland: Pilgrim, 2005.

Dube, Musa W. Shomanah. *Postcolonial Feminist Interpretation of the Bible*. St. Louis: Chalice, 2000.

Ellis, Wes. "Human Beings and Human Becomings: Departing from the Developmental Model of Youth Ministry." *Journal of Youth and Theology* 14, no. 2 (2015): 119–137.

Epstein, Robert. *Teen 2.0: Saving Our Children and Families from the Torment of Adolescence*. Fresno, CA: Quill Driver, 2010.

Erickson, Joseph A., and Susan E. O'Connor. "Service-Learning: Does It Promote or Reduce Prejudice?" In *Integrating Service Learning and Multicultural Education in Colleges and Universities*, edited by Carolyn R. O'Grady, 59–70. Mahwah, NJ: Lawrence Erlbaum, 2000.

Fass, Paula S. *The End of American Childhood: A History of Parenting from Life on the Frontier to the Managed Child*. Princeton, NJ: Princeton University Press, 2016.

Gatto, John Taylor. *Dumbing Us Down: The Hidden Curriculum of Compulsory Schooling*. 25th anniversary ed. Gabriola Island, BC: New Society, 2017.

Harrison, Beverly. "The Power of Anger in the Work of Love: Christian Ethics for Women and Other Strangers." *Union Seminary Quarterly Review* 36, no. 1 (1981): 41–57.

Hartman, Eric, Richard C. Kiely, Jessica Friedrichs, and Christopher Boettcher. *Community-Based Global Learning: The Theory and Practice of Ethical Engagement at Home and Abroad*. Sterling, VA: Stylus, 2018.

Hartman, Eric, Cody Morris Paris, and Brandon Blache-Cohen. "Fair Trade Learning: Ethical Standards for Community-Engaged International Volunteer Tourism." *Tourism and Hospitality Research* 14, nos. 1–2 (2014): 108–116. https://doi.org/10.1177/1467358414529443.

Hendricks, Obery M., Jr. *The Politics of Jesus: Rediscovering the True Revolutionary Nature of Jesus' Teachings and How They Have Been Corrupted*. New York: Doubleday, 2006.

Hine, Thomas. *The Rise and Fall of the American Teenager: A New History of the American Adolescent Experience*. New York: HarperCollins, 1999.

Holzer, Elie, and Orit Kent. *A Philosophy of Havruta: Understanding and Teaching the Art of Text Study in Pairs.* Brighton, MA: Academic Studies Press, 2013.

Horsley, Richard A. *Jesus and the Spiral of Violence: Popular Jewish Resistance in Roman Palestine.* San Francisco: Harper & Row, 1987.

Jacoby, Barbara, Gail Albert, Diana A. Bucco, Julie A. Busch, Sandra L. Enos, Irene S. Fischer, Catherine R. Gugerty, et al. *Service-Learning in Higher Education: Concepts and Practices.* San Francisco: Jossey-Bass, 1999.

Kent, Orit. "Interactive Text Study: A Case of *Hevruta* Learning." *Journal of Jewish Education* 72, no. 3 (2006): 205–232. https://doi.org/10.1080/15244110600990155.

———. "A Theory of *Havruta* Learning." *Journal of Jewish Education* 76, no. 3 (2010): 219–245. https://doi.org/10.1080/15244113.2010.501499.

Kett, Joseph F. *Rites of Passage: Adolescence in America 1790 to the Present.* New York: Basic Books, 1977.

Kwok, Pui-lan. *Discovering the Bible in the Non-biblical World.* Maryknoll, NY: Orbis, 1995.

Law, Eric. *The Wolf Shall Dwell with the Lamb: A Spirituality for Leadership in a Multicultural Community.* St. Louis: Chalice, 1993.

Lesko, Nancy. *Act Your Age! A Cultural Construction of Adolescence.* New York: Routledge Falmer, 2001.

Levine, Peter. *We Are the Ones We Have Been Waiting For: The Promise of Civic Renewal in America.* New York: Oxford University Press, 2013.

Linhart, Terence D. "They Were So Alive! The Spectacle Self and Youth Group Short-Term Mission Trips." *Missiology* 34, no. 4 (2006): 451–462.

Linklater, Richard, dir. *Dazed and Confused.* 1993; Universal City, CA: Gramercy Pictures, 1998. DVD.

Macy, Joanna. "Taking Heart: Spiritual Exercises from Social Activists." In *Peace Is the Way: Writings on Nonviolence from the Fellowship of Reconciliation*, edited by Walter Wink, 135–142. Maryknoll, NY: Orbis, 2000.

Marullo, Sam, and Bob Edwards. "From Charity to Justice: The Potential of University-Community Collaboration for Social Change." *American Behavioral Scientist* 43, no. 5 (2000): 895–912.

Metz, Johann Baptist. *Faith in History and Society: Toward a Practical Fundamental Theology.* New York: Seabury, 1980.

Miranda, Lin-Manuel. "Alexander Hamilton." MP3 audio. Track 1 on *Hamilton: An American Musical (Original Broadway Cast Recording).* Atlantic Records, 2015. tinyurl.com/4564vz2g.

———. "My Shot." MP3 audio. Track 3 on *Hamilton: An American Musical (Original Broadway Cast Recording).* Atlantic Records, 2015. tinyurl.com/4564vz2g.

Mitchell, Tania D. "Traditional vs. Critical Service-Learning: Engaging the Literature to Differentiate Two Models." *Michigan Journal of Community Service Learning* 14, no. 2 (2008): 50–65.

Mitchell, Tania D., David M. Donahue, and Courtney Young-Law. "Service-Learning as a Pedagogy of Whiteness." *Equity and Excellence in Education* 45, no. 4 (2012): 612–629.

Molnar-Main, Stacie. *Deliberation in the Classroom: Fostering Critical Thinking, Community, and Citizenship in Schools*. Ashland, OH: Kettering Foundation, 2017.

Morris, Monique W. *Pushout: The Criminalization of Black Girls in Schools*. New York: New Press, 2016.

Myers, Ched. *"Say to This Mountain": Mark's Story of Discipleship*. Maryknoll, NY: Orbis, 1996.

Myers, Jeremy, and Mark J. Jackson. "The Freedom of a Teenager: Vocation and Service Learning as the Future of Youth Ministry." *Dialog* 47, no. 4 (2008): 327–338.

Nagler, Michael N. *The Nonviolence Handbook: A Guide for Practical Action*. San Francisco: Berrett-Koehler, 2014.

Platt, Anthony M. *The Child Savers: The Invention of Delinquency*. Expanded 40th anniversary ed. New Brunswick, NJ: Rutgers University Press, 2009.

Rios, Victor M. *Punished: Policing the Lives of Black and Latino Boys*. New York: New York University Press, 2011.

Root, Andrew. "The Youth Ministry Mission Trip as Global Tourism: Are We OK with This?" *Dialog* 47, no. 4 (2008): 314–319.

Rosenberg, Marshall. *Nonviolent Communication: A Language of Life*. Encinitas, CA: PuddleDancer, 2003.

Rourke, Brad. *Developing Materials for Deliberative Forums*. Dayton, OH: Kettering Foundation, 2014. https://tinyurl.com/y37xa4bl.

Rynne, Terrence J. *Jesus Christ Peacemaker: A New Theology of Peace*. Maryknoll, NY: Orbis, 2015.

Savage, Jon. *Teenage: The Creation of Youth Culture*. New York: Penguin, 2007.

Schor, Juliet. *Born to Buy: The Commercialized Child and the New Consumer Culture*. New York: Scribner, 2004.

Scott, David W. *Crossing Boundaries: Sharing God's Good News through Mission*. Nashville: Wesley's Foundery, 2019.

Segovia, Fernando F., and Mary Ann Tolbert, eds. *Reading from This Place*. Vol. 1, *Social Location and Biblical Interpretation in the United States*. Minneapolis: Fortress, 1995.

Shargel, Rebecca. "*Havruta* Goes to the University: *Havruta*-Style Text Study in a College Education Class." *Journal of Jewish Education* 85, no. 1 (2019): 4–26. https://doi.org/10.1080/15244113.2019.1558385.

Sharp, Gene. *The Politics of Nonviolent Action*. Part 1, *Power and Struggle*. Boston: Porter Sargent, 1973.

———. *Waging Nonviolent Struggle: 20th Century Practice and 21st Century Potential*. Boston: Porter Sargent, 2005.

Sherr, Michael E., Diana R. Farland, and Terry A. Wolfer. "The Role of Community Service in the Faith Development of Adolescents." *Journal of Youth Ministry* 6, no. 1 (2007): 43–54.

Skocpol, Theda. *Diminished Democracy: From Membership to Management in American Civil Life*. Norman: University of Oklahoma Press, 2003.

Smith, Christian, and Melinda Lundquist Denton. *Soul Searching: The Religious and Spiritual Lives of American Teenagers*. New York: Oxford University Press, 2005.

Smith, James K. A. *Desiring the Kingdom: Worship, Worldview, and Cultural Formation*. Cultural Liturgies, vol. 1. Grand Rapids, MI: Baker Academic, 2009.

———. *You Are What You Love: The Spiritual Power of Habit*. Grand Rapids, MI: Brazos, 2016.

Stoecker, Randy. *Liberating Service Learning and the Rest of Higher Education Civic Engagement*. Philadelphia: Temple University Press, 2016.

Stone, Howard W., and James O. Duke. *How to Think Theologically*. 3rd ed. Minneapolis: Augsburg Fortress, 2013.

Stucky, Nathan. *Wrestling with Rest: Inviting Youth to Discover the Gift of Sabbath*. Grand Rapids, MI: Eerdmans, 2019.

Swartley, William M., ed. *The Love of Enemy and Nonretaliation in the New Testament*. Louisville, KY: Westminster John Knox, 1992.

Thomas, Angie. *The Hate U Give*. London: Walker, 2017.

Trinitapoli, Jenny, and Stephen Vaisey. "The Transformative Role of Religious Experience: The Case of Short-Term Missions." *Social Forces* 88, no. 1 (2009): 121–146.

Trocmé, André. *Jesus and the Nonviolent Revolution*. Edited by Charles Moore. Maryknoll, NY: Orbis, 2003.

White, David. *Practicing Discernment with Youth: A Transformative Youth Ministry Approach*. Cleveland: Pilgrim, 2005.

Wilson, Patricia A. "Deep Democracy: The Inner Practice of Civic Engagement." *Fieldnotes: A Newsletter of the Shambala Institute*, no. 3 (February 2004): 1–6.

Wink, Walter. *Engaging the Powers: Discernment and Resistance in a World of Domination*. Minneapolis: Fortress, 1992.

———. *The Powers That Be: Theology for a New Millennium*. New York: Doubleday, 1999.

Wright, Almeda M. *The Spiritual Lives of Young African Americans*. Oxford: Oxford University Press, 2017.

Yoder, John Howard. *The Politics of Jesus: Vicut Agnus Noster*. 2nd ed. Grand Rapids, MI: Eerdmans, 1994.

Young, Iris Marion. *Justice and the Politics of Difference*. Princeton, NJ: Princeton University Press, 2012.